THINKING
OUTSIDE
THE BOOK

THINKING OUTSIDE THE BOOK

Alternatives for Today's Teen Library Collections

Edited by C. ALLEN NICHOLS

Libraries Unlimited Professional Guides for Young Adult Librarians Series
C. Allen Nichols and Mary Anne Nichols, Series Editors

A Member of the Greenwood Publishing Group

Westport, Connecticut • London

Library of Congress Cataloging-in-Publication Data

Thinking outside the book : alternatives for today's teen library collections / edited by
C. Allen Nichols.
    p. cm.—(Libraries Unlimited professional guides for young adult librarians
series, ISSN 1532–5571)
  Includes bibliographical references (p.) and index.
  ISBN 1–59158–059–5 (alk. paper)
  1. Young adults' libraries—Collection development—United States. 2. Libraries—
Special collections—Nonbook materials. 3. Multimedia library services—United
States. 4. Libraries and teenagers—United States. I. Nichols, C. Allen. II. Libraries
Unlimited professional guides for young adult librarians.
  Z718.5.T47 2004
  027.62'6—dc22   2003060592

British Library Cataloguing in Publication Data is available.

Library of Congress Catalog Card Number: 2003060592
ISBN: 1–59158–059–5
ISSN: 1532–5571

First published in 2004

Libraries Unlimited, 88 Post Road West, Westport, CT 06881
A Member of the Greenwood Publishing Group, Inc.
www.lu.com

Printed in the United States of America

The paper used in this book complies with the
Permanent Paper Standard issued by the National
Information Standards Organization (Z39.48–1984).

10 9 8 7 6 5 4 3 2 1

Copyright Acknowledgments

The editor and publisher gratefully acknowledge permission for use of the following
materials:

Selected Lists of Audiobooks for Young Adults produced by the YALSA Media Selection
and Usage Committee, now known as the Audio Book and Alternative Media Exploration
Committee for the years 1999–2003 used with permission.

All images are reproduced with permission of Demco, Inc.

This book is dedicated to my loving family.
They are the reason I exist—Mary Anne, Evan, and Bennett.

CONTENTS

ILLUSTRATIONS

SERIES FOREWORD

We firmly believe in young adult library services, and advocate for teens whenever we can. We are proud of our association with Libraries Unlimited and Greenwood Publishing Group, and grateful for their acknowledgment of the need for additional resources for teen-serving librarians. We intend for this series to fill those needs, providing useful and practical handbooks for library staff. Readers will find some theory and philosophical musings, but for the most part, this series will focus on real-life library issues with answers and suggestions for front-line librarians.

Our passion for young adult librarian services continues to reach new peaks. As we travel to present workshops on the various facets of working with teens in public libraries, we are encouraged by the desire of librarians everywhere to learn what they can do in their libraries to make teens welcome. This is a positive sign, since too often libraries choose to ignore this underserved group of patrons. We hope you find this series to be a useful tool in fostering your own enthusiasm for teens.

Mary Anne Nichols
C. Allen Nichols
Series Editors

PREFACE

For me *Thinking Outside the Book* started as a project that I was advising another editor on, but when he had to step aside for personal reasons, I jumped in and began working to pull it together. I've learned a great deal from the experience, and I believe you will too as you read the pages that follow.

I would like to address a couple of points before you start reading. The first is the use of the term "young adult" (YA) versus the term "teen." Since this is a compilation of contributions from several different writers, both terms are used interchangeably throughout the book. I spent a great deal of time considering the use of one term over the other, but concluded that it doesn't matter. The use of both simply reflects the continued use of both within the profession.

The Young Adult Library Services Association (YALSA), a division of the American Library Association (ALA), obviously uses the term young adult. YALSA defines a young adult as someone between the ages of twelve and eighteen. As I write this, I have considered the recent discussion among YALSA's Board of Directors regarding changing the organization's name. At its 2003 Midwinter meeting, the Board concluded that the term young adult is appropriate because it is a term used for an audience within the profession. While it doesn't convey the term's meaning to those outside the profession, that is not its purpose.

A couple of years ago I changed the name of the young adult department and the title of the young adult librarian at the Wadsworth Public Library, where I am director, to teen services. For me, our primary customers are the teens in our community, not other professionals. This has worked well for us as we communicate our services and programs to those teens.

I am grateful that David Serchay and Tracey Firestone made the commitment to stay on with this project through the editorial transition.

Many people working in the field of teen services are familiar with Tracey because of her success as the Webmaster for the Young Adult Librarians' Homepage. She is the Young Adult Specialist for the Suffolk Cooperative Library System, in Bellport, New York. She works with the 55 independent libraries in Suffolk County to improve and expand library services for teenaged patrons. An advocate for the expansion of library services on the Web, Tracey is one of Suffolk County's Live Librarians, offering live chat reference assistance. She is also the Webmaster for the Virtual YA Index: Public Libraries with Young Adult Web Pages and for the New York Library Association's Youth Services Section, and is the chair of YALSA's Teen Web Advisory Committee.

David is a youth services librarian for the Broward County (FL) Library System. He has written on comics and graphic novels for a number of publications including *Library Journal*, *Comics Source*, *Animato*, and *Serials Review*. He has been reading comic books for most of his life and has a personal collection of over 18,000 comics, dating back over 40 years. On-line, he is a "founding member" of GN-LIB (a list for those interested in graphic novels and libraries), and a longtime participant in the Grand Comic Database Project (http://www.comics.org), an international on-line group dedicated to cataloging every comic book ever made. He can be reached at dserchay@yahoo.com.

Three of the additional authors are relatively new to the library field—but all have great potential. Two of them were students at the Kent State University School of Library and Information Science when I met them in a workshop that my wife and I teach. Kevin Ferst and Christine Borne graduated and have jobs as librarians—Kevin in Jacksonville, Florida and Christine in Shaker Heights, Ohio.

The other new librarian is already demonstrating her potential. I can say this because she works at "my" library. Valerie A. Ott is the Teen Services Librarian at Wadsworth Public Library in Wadsworth, Ohio. She earned a bachelor's degree in English from Xavier University in 1998 and a master's degree in library and information science from Kent State University in 2001. Valerie is a member of the Ohio Library Council, ALA, and YALSA. As our Teen Services Librarian, she is the administrator of a grant aimed at promoting financial literacy to teens funded by the Drew Carey Grant for Young Adult Services in Ohio. In addition, Valerie facilitates an active teen advisory board and an annual summer reading program, and leads several after-school programs.

The other contributors to this book have already proven themselves in the field, and continue to advocate for teens. Sarah Flowers is a librarian for the Santa Clara County Library in California. She served four years on YALSA's Best DVDs and Videos for Young Adults Committee. She currently writes the "Teen Screen" video review column for *Voice of Youth Advocates* (*VOYA*). She lives in Morgan Hill, California with her husband, and has three grown sons.

Francisca Goldsmith has coordinated Teen Services at Berkeley (CA) Public Library since 1992. The collections and programs at Berkeley Public Library include spoken word recordings targeting teens of diverse interests and needs in multiple formats. She is a past chair of YALSA's Audio Book and Media Exploration (formerly Media Selection and Usage) Committee.

Lastly, Melanie Rapp-Weiss was the easiest arm to twist. During her life as a graduate library school student, she completed a practicum experience with me when I was employed by the Cuyahoga County Public Library. She has been working in libraries for fifteen years in various exciting positions, including driving a bookmobile. From Montana, she left the Big Sky in 1995 to earn an MLS from Kent State University. She is now a Regional Teen Services Manager for Cuyahoga County Public Library. She was the 2002–2003 Chair of YALSA's Quick Picks for Reluctant Young Adult Readers Committee.

Thank you to each of the contributors. Without the hard work of each, not to mention the dedication to teens and libraries that each possesses, this book would still be waiting to be published.

ACKNOWLEDGMENTS

The editor gratefully acknowledges the permission of the following to use copyrighted materials in this book: Janet Nelson from DEMCO, Inc. for the permission to reproduce each of the photographs included in this book. In addition to the permission to use the photos, DEMCO was kind enough to provide a copy of each on disk to facilitate their use. The photographs can be found on DEMCO's Web site (http://www.demco.com), as well as in its 2003 Annual Catalog. The Young Adult Library Services Association, a division of the American Library Association, for the permission to reproduce copies of its Selected Lists of Audiobooks for Young Adults.

INTRODUCTION

For years, even centuries, the word "library" was equated with the word "books." Periodicals were the only real exception, until film, film-strips, and slides came along, and a few libraries established collections for those "nonprint media." Then, in the latter half of the 20th century, an explosion of audio recordings, then video recordings brought tremendous change to the library. The importance of these changes was reflected through the needs of our customers. While librarians were sometimes slow to add these new formats to their collections, our customers did not hesitate to amass large collections. They created personal collections of new formats and bypassed the library in doing so. Once the demand became undeniable, libraries added the formats, but they found they had already lost many customers.

Libraries can't afford to continue to behave this way—especially when it comes to their teen customers. Today's teens don't automatically turn to the library for research and reference needs as young people did 20 years ago when I was a teen. "In the old days," libraries could depend on a steady stream of teens doing homework, research, and so on. Now the traffic has slowed because the Internet has lured teens into a venue that is much more appealing to them than the dusty/musty neighborhood library.

As a result, teen librarians must look for new ways to create a flow of teens inside their buildings. One way to do that is to provide a variety of formats, collected specifically for teens, in spaces teens can identify as their own. That is what this book is about.

In her book *Radical Change: Books for Youth in a Digital Age*, Eliza Dresang tells us that readers are no longer stimulated simply by the "standard" format of the written word. Since this is the case, I believe it is vitally important for libraries to provide alternative materials to the "standard book" that will stimulate and appeal to teens. It is important to have the types of materials she suggests in order to help the teens of the "Internet-generation," but the teen library collection shouldn't just stop there. It should also embrace a wide variety of alternative formats to further stimulate those teens. The library should become a place where teens can explore the latest popular formats. That is what this book is about.

When discussing alternative and new formats, oftentimes I hear the cries of "We don't have enough space," or "We don't have enough money." I don't buy any of these arguments.

Yes, lack of space is a problem, and so is a lack of funds. However, it has been my experience that many librarians, or in particular library directors, can work around these issues by establishing a set of priorities. Too often, library staff are afraid of making the hard choices necessary to provide teens with what teens need and want. One of the problems is that teens are underserved and sometimes undesired. The last thing many non–young adult librarians want is a group of teens "invading" their quiet library. So it's easier to use space and funding as excuses than to try to resolve a problem that disenfranchises teens from using the library. The other problem to overcome is that, in my belief, there are many librarians who value "the book" to a point where they are almost elitist in their view of other formats—more on this later.

There is little in the literature that discusses these materials in a way that allows librarians to easily examine the information from the collection development perspective. Also, this book gathers together—in a single location—information on each of its topics. This effort frees the hectic librarian who doesn't have the time to keep up with all the challenges that face teen services in today's rapidly changing technological world. More importantly, this book provides the information necessary to build support for the inclusion of these items in the library collection to counteract the problems mentioned above.

This book examines the facets of teen collection development for the following types of materials:

- Magazines
- Graphic novels and comic books
- Audiobooks
- Music
- Videos
- Web sites/on-line collections
- Game- and CD-ROM–based reference sources

When you "think outside the book," these are the significant alternative formats that exist today—and every teen knows about them. This book also contains a chapter on furnishings to use within the teen space. It is my opinion that it is no longer "enough" to just collect and house materials that teens (or anyone else) might like. Merchandising is a necessity to appropriately market to teens and entice them to pick up, examine, review, and ultimately check out the collections libraries build for them.

This book's topics are arranged in the order listed above. This order was selected as a logical (to me anyway) order as you move from the written word found in a book. Each chapter provides background information on each format, as well as reviewing sources, selection criteria, challenges to expect/overcome, recommended titles to collect, and purchasing information.

While the formats discussed in this book aren't new, there are still libraries that don't have one, or more likely, more than one of these formats in their teen collections (assuming they have a teen collection at all).

I hope this book will provide some help to those teen-serving library employees who are interested in encouraging teens to use their library. This book is written not solely for the teen librarian. In most cases, library "generalists," MLS-degreed or not, serve teens on a daily basis. This book is for them as well. Because too few libraries have teen librarians on staff, these "generalists" serve far more teens than do teen librarians. It is especially important that these teen-serving library employees be provided with as much support material as possible. I believe this book fulfills that role. My passion as a former young adult librarian, and now as a teen advocate, is to encourage teens to read—anything. So I ask myself, why am I working on this book? The answer is simple; in order to draw teens into the library, you need these materials. Once you have teens in your building, then you have a chance to lead them to the written word.

That, however, should not be your ultimate goal. There are many teens who may never turn to the written word, but yet, they need library services and collections just as much, if not more, than do those who like books. They need to know that the library is as much for them as it is for anyone else. Having these alternatives in your collections will help them learn that is the case. What better ideal can there be in this day and age of busy schedules and the Internet than making the library and its collection as easy, exciting, and accessible as the Internet? If you can achieve this, teens will remember the positive experiences they had in your library. That is vitally important as they grow older and, if you have laid the groundwork, become the ubiquitous life-long user. I believe this book will help you achieve that goal and ultimately instill the love of libraries in your customers. That is what this book is about.

1

ZINES FOR TEENS

Christine Borne and Kevin Ferst

Developing a magazine collection is a fantastic way to successfully serve your finicky teen population. Let's face it: books are for geeks. At least, that's what many teens think. Whereas your average multiple-pierced, pink-haired kid might not be caught dead reading the most recent Printz Award winner, he or she may be eagerly waiting for this month's issue of *SPIN*.

There are many reasons to develop a teen magazine collection. In this chapter, we will discuss other issues of importance as listed below.

- Types of magazines
- Beginning a magazine collection
- Advantages, disadvantages, and points to consider
- Sources for purchasing magazines
- Marketing and display options
- Collection development resources

Magazines can fulfill teens' evolving developmental, informational, educational, and recreational needs. Here are some starter points for why developing a magazine collection can help address the needs of your teen patrons:

- *Timeliness.* Books take a long time to write and can easily become ancient history to your time-sensitive teen population. Take, for example, the cover of Joan Bauer's *Hope Was Here*, published in 2000, which depicts the pre-9/11 New York skyline. Magazines, on the other hand, have their finger on the pulse of pop culture. Some are published every week, and in the case of on-line magazines, can be "published" or updated every day. This is the kind of currency teens demand, and without it, they can become easily bored.

- *Short Takes.* Teens short on attention and free time may find that books just have too slow a tempo to be satisfactorily stimulating. We challenge you to flip through any teen magazine and find ten articles that take you more than a couple of minutes to read. Short articles with no-frills vocabulary and glitzy, eye-catching graphics are perfect for teens too busy to read books, but hungry for intellectual stimulation. Layout is also important, allowing kids' eyes to jump from one news or "information byte" to another, lingering on whatever they might find of particular interest in any given moment. In recent years, some teen books have dramatically changed in style, trying to emulate a more technological, Internet-like feel. This development is known as *Radical Change*, and is described in the book of the same title by Eliza Dresang.

- *Matching Niche Interests.* While magazines can cover an array of general topics of interest to teens, their ability to focus on specific areas is one of their greatest assets. Magazines can thrive on delivering specialized and timely content unlikely to appear in books. Teens beginning to develop specialized areas of interest may have to turn to magazines to meet these unique needs.

- *Less "Uncool" Than Books.* Ask a teen if they like to read, and you may be answered with a curled lip and a shake of the head. Ten minutes later, those same kids will be chillin' on the couch with the latest *GamePro* or *Animerica*. For whatever reason, there is something stigmatizing and nerdish about books and not their glossy, staple-bound cousins. Magazines, with their leaner girth and paperback format, can be suitably tucked in a back pocket without any peer backlash, as opposed to a clumsy hardbound tome.

TYPES OF MAGAZINES

There are three general types of magazines we'll talk about—print, on-line, and zines.

Print

This is the "traditional" format. Generally, print magazines fall into two categories. First, there are magazines specifically written for and marketed to teens, such as *Teen People*, and *Teen Ink* (which is written by teens for teens). These may vary in content from covering the latest fads and gossip, like "what's Lil Bow Wow listening to on the tour bus?" to more serious topics such as date rape and pregnancy. Some titles, such as *Word Up!*, are filled with glossy pictures and posters of teen idols.

Secondly, there are magazines marketed to college-age or adult audiences that also have high teen appeal, such as *The Source*, *Thrasher*, and *PC Gamer*. You may want to consider some of these for content that would interest your particular population. For example, *Mother Jones*, *Vegetarian Times*, *Clamor*, and *Utne Reader* may be good selections for teens who show an interest in social activism. Special interest magazines, such as *Cooking Light* or *Car and Driver*, could appeal to teens training in vocational schools.

On-line Magazines

Some on-line magazines are simply on-line counterparts to traditional magazines. Others are Web-only periodicals, which can satisfy very specific interests. The downside is that they may come and go with no warning. If you are going to link on-line magazines to your teen page, make sure you have a maintenance plan. You could very well appoint a "Web committee" on your Teen Advisory Board (TAB), or at least have one of your teens check every month or so to see if the links are still active.

Zines

Zines, originally short for "fanzines," are handmade, usually not-for-profit publications that generally serve as a creative outlet for their writers. Zines may be crudely photocopied, hand-stapled, local productions or they can be more professionally done and internationally distributed. They are the smallest of the small presses, and can be the most difficult to find out about and keep track of. Anyone can make a zine, including your own teen patrons: so if you're running out of programming ideas, try a zine workshop!

BEGINNING A MAGAZINE COLLECTION

Don't Forget...

One of the easiest and most useful ways to determine which magazines to include in your collection is to ask the teens themselves.

One of the easiest and most useful ways to determine which magazines to include in your collection is to ask the teens themselves. Since the teens are the ones who will be using the collection, it only makes sense to get your information directly from them. You can do this either informally through talking with your teen patrons and working with your TAB, or by conducting a formal reader interest survey (or informal: try displaying a dry-erase marker board with the message: "write your favorite magazines here!" in your teen area). We think doing all of these things is best! Not only will getting the information directly from your teens give you the information most relevant to your specific teenage population, but you will also be providing teens a valuable chance to meaningfully participate in their community, which reinforces to them that their patronage is a valuable asset to your library.

By allowing teens to participate, librarians are saying "yes" to *positive youth development*, the emerging philosophy of youth services that supports the broader developmental needs of youth. The idea is to give teens a chance to play a role in all areas of teen services. Collaborative collection development also makes life slightly easier for the librarian, because you're not the only one brainstorming. For more details on Positive Youth Development, see *New Directions for Library Services to Young Adults*, by Patrick Jones.

Factors to Consider

In order to develop a broad picture of the different areas of interest that teens in your community have, consider the following as they relate to teens:

- Groups and Clubs
- Sports
- Special Interests
- Teen Culture
- Community Demographics
- Educational and Developmental Opportunities

If you have a TAB, you already have the perfect vehicle for planning your magazine collection. You can begin by asking for suggestions of which magazines they like. Try to find out not just the particular interests of your TAB members, but what other teens in the community like. Bring some sample magazines to your TAB meetings and have a vote. Try to get a broad picture of all the different areas of interest that teens in your community have, and ask lots of questions. There are so many different types of magazines; nearly every interest can be matched to a publication. When conducting your community analysis, remember these points:

- *Groups and Clubs.* Find out what kinds of groups and clubs exist in your school and community service area, such as art and performance groups, computer/Internet groups, environmental groups, foreign language clubs, newspaper and writing groups, and youth government clubs.
- *Sports.* What types of sports are represented in your schools? Many good general magazines for sports exist, such as *Sports Illustrated*, as well as publications for particular sports, often split by gender. Think of some common sports, like baseball, basketball, and martial arts, plus some of the more unusual sports that members of your community may participate in.
- *Special Interests.* Magazines thrive on delivering specialized content. It seems as if magazines exist for nearly every interest out

there, like role-playing games, science fiction, poetry, pro wrestling, and video and computer games. Each interest can likely be broken down into even more particular interests, such as video games for specific systems, like *Nintendo Power* for the Nintendo Game Cube system, versus *Electronic Gaming Monthly*, a more general gaming magazine.

- *Culture.* This is a big one. Be sure to focus in areas of music popular in your community, as well as general pop culture, celebrities, and movies.

- *Community Demographics.* What kinds of kids live in your community? Try to think of all the different types of demographics that exist, such as race, nationality, sexual orientation, political affiliations, and religious background. For example, if 95 percent of the teen girls who use your collection are African American, you might want to get *Black Hairstyles and Trends Magazine* instead of *Teen Hairstyles*, which primarily depicts white teens. Also, think of the appeal factor of different subgroups in your community, such as Goths, neo-hippies, punks, or straight edge.

- *Educational/Developmental.* While teens enjoy magazines because they are entertaining, magazines can also be very informative. Not only are there magazines devoted to helping teens think about colleges and careers, but also many have articles that can help teens develop their sense of identity and independence.

Once you have defined the scope of interests teens in your community have, you can begin the process of trying to match up interests with publications. You'll have to decide what kinds of publications you want—print, on-line, zine, or a mix of all three.

To gain an understanding of some of the magazines available, do some field research in your community. Visit your local bookstore and see what magazines they have, which ones the teens are browsing, and which ones seem to be selling well. You might even want to ask the manager which titles get stolen most often (not to imply that they are all stolen by teens, of course!). Some of the larger bookstores like Borders and Barnes & Noble have extensive magazine collections that represent a diverse array of interests. Bring a notepad and write down some ideas. Don't forget to note any material that your community might find objectionable—you want to be as familiar as possible with the content, in case someone challenges it later on.

Once you're back at the reference desk, you can go on-line to see if the magazines on your list have Web sites. Sometimes, magazine Web sites even contain full-text articles from their print equivalent for free. Even if there aren't full-text articles, you can still develop a feel for what the magazine is like.

In your community there are a multitude of places that distribute magazines of general and special teen interest. Try specialty stores, like skateboarding or bike shops; specialty music stores; clothing stores; coffee shops; and concert clubs. Locally owned stores might also be great places to discover locally produced zines. Even if a store doesn't sell magazines, maybe the teens hanging out there are reading their own, or talking about it or their interests. The general rule is—always keep your eyes and ears open!

Another easy way to garner ideas of what to select for your teen magazine collection is to see what teens already are reading from your library's general magazine collection. Chances are that they have already been using the main collection to check out the copies of such popular magazines as *Sports Illustrated*, *Elle*, *Hot Rod*, and *People*. Observe which titles they pick up most often, and buy an extra copy for your teen collection.

Helpful Hint

Don't forget to review your circulation statistics to determine which titles in your existing collection are most popular.

For on-line magazines, take what topics of interest you have gathered from your reader interest surveys and TAB, and do some searching to see if any on-line publications exist. This will also help you find out the existence of traditional magazines. You will be surprised at how many publications exist! Try on-line directories such as Yahoo!, Open Source Directory Project, and Zeal. See the section on *Collection Development Resources* below for more details. Also, find out what everyone else is doing! Visit teen magazine collections at other libraries and write down some titles. Compare their community demographics to yours. There are a number of titles, such as *Seventeen*, that probably every teen magazine collection should own. Visiting a number of other libraries will give you a good idea of what these core titles are. Once you develop a magazine collection, be sure to give the teens a chance to have continued input into the evaluation of your collection.

Finally, a word to the wise: Magazines have a tendency to be short-lived. Titles come, go, and evolve into different entities with little or no warning. Always be on the lookout for new publications, and be ready to drop the ones that cover waning fads and interests.

ADVANTAGES, DISADVANTAGES, AND POINTS TO CONSIDER

Magazines can be a great addition to your teen collection, but they can create particular challenges for you. Here are some points you might want to consider:

- *Disposable vs. Permanent.* Are you an archivist or are you a maven of pop culture? The truth is, teen magazines can and probably will get trashed. They don't look very good after having been crammed into a dozen or more backpacks. If your teen magazines look pristine, you might want to check if anyone is actually reading them. Plus, fanzines like *Word Up!* will undoubtedly have pictures ripped out (and the posters, too, if you don't get to them first!). So, you may want to accept them as ephemera and stop trying to house *Seventeen* all the way back to 1996!

- *Space.* Do you have the space to store your magazine collection, and if you do, where is it located? Face-out shelving is, of course, best for magazines. Do you have a magazine rack? Is it in a place where teens can see it, and is there a place for them to sit down nearby, both alone and in groups?

- *Intellectual Freedom.* In 1996, the Council of the American Library Association reaffirmed the inclusion of "age" in the Library Bill of Rights point five, that "A person's right to use a library should not be denied or abridged because of origin, age, background, or views." However, you will need to keep in mind that if you select titles marketed to adults, like *Sports Illustrated*, or *SPIN*, they may contain more potentially controversial adult-oriented content, including racy covers, sex-based advertising, and coverage of "taboo" topics. As an extreme example, *SPIN*, in a 1988 issue, inserted a free condom inside the magazine itself. Be aware of the possible challenges you may face, and be prepared to meet them.

- *Open vs. Restricted Access.* Some libraries, in order to curb theft, prefer to keep the current copy of certain popular magazines at the reference desk. While this might work as theft prevention, it might also simply keep teens from using your collection. If you subscribe to the "disposable" theory, theft might not be a big deal. If you have a security system, consider inserting security strips in magazines as well as books (some libraries do, some don't).

- *Will You Let Them Circulate?* This might depend on how pristine you want their condition to remain. But remember, magazines can boost circulation statistics.

- *How Often Does Your Collection Development Policy Allow You to Renew or Discontinue Titles? Can You Cancel Titles Mid-year If They Flop?* You might get stuck with a two-year subscription to *Nintendo Power* long after Nintendo has ceased to be cool. Then, not only are you wasting money and space, you're losing face with your teen patrons by having "unhip" magazines.

- *The Pains of Claiming.* What happens if you never receive the October *Teen People*? Will you bother to claim it, or just let it go, figuring that by the time it arrives, no one will care about Josh Hartnett anymore? The issue depends on your preferences, plus the scope of your responsibilities (i.e., whether you have a Technical Services department, or whether you're all you've got).

- *Less Control for On-line.* To some, it's easier to thumb through some traditional print magazines to see if the magazine is something you want for your teen area. But ever-changing on-line magazines are a different story. On-line resources offer you the least control, so be sure to select your sources carefully, and periodically check to see that the content is still what you want.

- *Privacy.* Teens can be assured a certain level of privacy by utilizing on-line resources because there's no chance of "getting caught" with book in hand by parents who might freak out. Zines may be more transient, and obviously, their content is difficult/impossible to archive.

WHERE DO MAGAZINES COME FROM? THE PROCESS, SIMPLIFIED

This is probably no surprise, but the magazines you buy at the newsstand don't arrive directly from the publisher. That would be too complicated for your local newsagent. They would potentially have to deal with dozens of individual publishers. Of course, business has evolved to make the process much easier. Retailers (bookstores, newsstands, supermarkets) purchase their magazine supplies through a wholesaler, whether it be a large company, such as *International Periodical Distribution,* or a more geographically specific one, such as *Empire State News Company,* whose job it is to deal with the individual publishers so that the retailer doesn't have to. Libraries and other non-retail entities generally purchase their magazines from jobbers or subscription services, the most popular of which is EBSCO.

Most likely, you will purchase your magazines from magazine jobbers, newsstands, or a combination of both. You may also purchase from wholesalers, the agents who supply to local newsstands. The following is a discussion of what each can (and can't!) do for the library.

Useful Information

A fairly comprehensive list of magazine jobbers is available at the Iowa Library Services Areas Web site at http://www.ilsa.lib.ia.us/magjobs.html (unfortunately, this page does not list jobbers' Web addresses). You may also want to look under "Periodical Suppliers" in the latest issue of *Librarians Yellow Pages* (available either in print or on-line at http://www.librariansyellowpages.com).

Magazine Jobbers

Don't cut out the middleman! A magazine jobber, otherwise known as a subscription service, is a wholesaler that sells magazine and other periodical subscriptions only to retailers and institutions. They are the liaison between the publishers and the libraries, so to speak. Using a jobber means you don't have to fill out a million little subscription cards and keep track yourself of when they are going to run out.

Some Magazine Jobbers of Note

EBSCO Subscription Services
P.O. Box 1943
Birmingham, AL 35201-1943
Phone: (205) 991-6600

Fax: (205) 995-1518

http://www-us.ebsco.com/home/printsubs/default.asp

(see http://www-us.ebsco.com/home/contact/northam.asp for all regional offices in North America)

EBSCO Subscription Services is a division of EBSCO Information Services, a corporation that delivers print and on-line periodical subscriptions, databases, and even books to all kinds of libraries. EBSCO Subscription Services deals with (you guessed it!) periodical subscriptions. Check out Related Services for Public Libraries and Related Services for K–12 on the above Web site.

One of the most useful features of EBSCO is its Missing Copy Bank—a two-year backfile of periodicals from which they provide free replacements for any missing issues you might have. Although this isn't as important with teen magazines as it is with an academic collection, especially if you view teen magazines as essentially disposable, free stuff is never, ever bad. EBSCO also makes available over 4,000 periodical titles in Spanish, and has some budgeting and price forecasting features.

DEMCO

Attn: Periodicals Department

P.O. Box 7760

Madison, WI 53707-7760

Phone: (800) 962-4463

Fax: (800) 245-1329

http://www.demco.com

DEMCO offers periodical subscription service, library furniture, book repair and other library supplies, and educational materials. Although plenty of adult titles are available, DEMCO is generally oriented toward the K-12 set, and may be a better choice than EBSCO for school libraries.

Wolper Subscription Services, Inc.

6 Centre Square

Suite 202

Easton, PA 18042-3691

Phone: (610) 559-9550

Fax: (610) 559-9898

http://www.wolper.com

Wolper's title database contains over 250,000 serials including domestic and foreign publications, newspapers, e-journals and on-line publications, directories, annuals, and multimedia products.

W.T. Cox Subscriptions, Inc.
201 Village Road
Shallotte, NC 28470-4441
Phone: (800) 571-9554
Fax: (910) 755-6274
http://www.wtcox.com

W.T. Cox maintains access to over 250,000 journals and periodicals and approximately 1,000 CD-ROMs or electronic format products. Its annual catalog lists 3,000 of the most frequently ordered periodicals and CD-ROMs.

Pros of Using Jobbers

- Purchasing from one place streamlines operations. This is a *big* deal if your library subscribes to more than a handful of magazines!
- You sometimes get discounts this way. Make sure to ask!

Cons of Using Jobbers

- Even the biggest of mega-jobbers won't carry everything. Something that you see at the drugstore may not be available through EBSCO. A smaller or less lucrative periodical that becomes very popular in your library might be discontinued by the jobber mid-year. If your acquisitions department wants to purchase magazines only from jobbers, there goes your popular magazine.
- Getting magazines this way might be slower than getting them from the newsstand.

Local Newsstands

If you live in a smaller community, getting to know your local news-agents might benefit you more than ordering through DEMCO or other subscription services. Check your local yellow pages for magazine retailers (try looking under "news dealers" or "magazines").

Pros of Using Local Newsstands

- You might be able to get smaller, local publications this way.
- You may be able to get them closer to their date of publication than you would through a subscription service.
- If you are going to have only a few magazines, this might be easier than dealing with Wolpert or another magazine supplier.
- Supporting local businesses is also never, ever bad!

Cons of Using Local Newsstands

- Chances are, someone from the library will have to go out and pick up the magazines, whether on library time or their own time. Talk to your newsagent; you may be able to arrange something.
- Unless you negotiate a discount with your newsagent, you will likely have to pay the cover price.

Wholesalers

As described above, wholesalers are the entities that supply magazines to retail outlets. Although generally libraries use jobbers such as EBSCO or W.T. Cox, you may wish to do otherwise.

If You Are Interested In . . .

Using a wholesaler, try contacting International Periodical Distributors, the largest direct-to-retail magazine distributor in the United States, at the following address:

IPD
Attn: IPD New Accounts
6195 Lusk Boulevard
San Diego, CA 92121-2729
Phone: (866) 473-4800 x538
Fax: (858) 677-3235

Pros of Using Wholesalers

- If you are going to let current issues circulate immediately, you can use a magazine wholesaler to get the issue to you quicker than a subscription agent would.

Cons of Using Wholesalers

• If you are already doing most of your business through a magazine jobber, the additional use of a wholesaler can complicate
your process. Make sure to discuss all aspects of the issue with
your acquisitions department, collection development committee,
and/or person in charge of ordering periodicals.

MARKETING AND DISPLAY OPTIONS

Once you have started a teen magazine collection consisting of a good
mix of traditional, on-line, and zine publications—it's time to get the
word out to the teens! This is a tremendous opportunity to reach out to
a whole new untapped teen audience that may never have considered
coming to your library before. The positive public relations you can build
through this can help you and your library for years to come in all areas
of library services.

A great way to start is to be sure to have an attractive and easily
accessible storage unit in which to display your new magazines. There
are many different kinds of shelving units, available from a variety of
distributors, such as DEMCO, Brodart, and Library Display Shelving.
Units come in all shapes and sizes, and can be made from a variety of
materials, including acrylic, aluminum, steel, plastic, and wood. Whatever you select, we suggest trying to utilize face-out shelving of some
kind, to let those flashy, attractive magazine covers advertise themselves!
Face-out shelving also enables easier browsing and accessibility. The following pages describe a few units we recommend to help you display
and store your collection. Photographs of the items are reproduced in
chapter 8.

Figure 8.1 is a Compact Magazine Spinner, which is separated into 16
pockets that hold 13 magazines each. It holds over 200 magazines in all.

The Durham Con-Tur Steel Literature Rack (Figure 8.2) is composed
of five individual racks that can be added together for expansion. Each
of these racks holds 23 titles.

Figure 8.3 is an end-of-range magazine display unit. It can fit at the
ends of your book ranges. Each of the eight pockets can hold nineteen
magazines.

A compartmentalized shelving system can display the current issue of
each magazine on a flip-up lid, while containing the back issues in a
compartment behind the lid. Figure 8.4 provides a sample of such a
system.

Of course, your major limitations will be budget and space, so see what they will allow. You can even use cheap wire or cardboard comic book displays for magazines. It's important to make sure that the area is kept looking decent. Magazines that are in the wrong place, empty display racks, and ripped covers do not invite teens to browse your collection!

The best way to spread the word and let teens know about your collection is to use the process you used to start your collection—use the teens themselves. As with anything else, word-of-mouth is still one of the most effective means of advertising. Encourage your TAB to promote your collections in their schools. Be sure to make special note of your new collection on all your current marketing vehicles, such as your newsletter, Web site, and database of teen patrons. Send out notices to schools and other partners in the community that work with your teens. Put up posters in teen hangouts, or better yet, have your teen volunteers do it— not only does this save you a trip, but it is more positive reinforcement of positive youth development. Also, if you picked titles based on specific user groups in your community, be sure to let them know about it! Send out notices to whatever group you've targeted, be they church groups, social groups, school clubs, sport teams, or special interest groups.

Be sure to market your magazine collection during your regular outreach procedures, such as your school visits, booktalk tours, and programs. Bring copies of all your new magazines and let the teens ogle! This is certain to bring in new users to your library. You can even do a special program or series of programs specifically designed to promote your new collection. You could have a magazine "opening night" party where you kick off your new collection; just be sure to have plenty of pizza. Perhaps you could have a contest promotion to name the new magazine center, or have the kids make special decorations. The possibilities are limitless.

Consider grouping certain subjects of magazines together, and marketing them with other materials. For example, group your music magazines by your CDs, or video game magazines by books about video games. Mix and match your media together and set up an attractive display. You can use this approach when you booktalk, too. Try *Ender's Game* (book and audiobook), *Starlog* magazine, some nice sci-fi graphic novels, and the soundtrack to *Star Wars*. Point out a few good science fiction Web sites while you're at it.

Prepare to have your magazines heavily used, torn up, beat up, and pulled or ripped apart. It's important to realize that magazines are much like convenience food—they fill a quick, temporary need. They are not designed to be a part of your permanent collection. So you can view your "casualties" as a sign of marketing well done. Be sure to recycle what you can! Old magazines are a great source of free posters and display materials that will ensure continued awareness of your super magazine collection. And, of course, revise, weed, and get feedback from the teens on new magazines to try out and which ones to drop off. Freshness and currency is in itself a great marketing tool.

COLLECTION DEVELOPMENT RESOURCES

Books and Magazine/Journal Articles

Here are some additional resources to check when developing a magazine collection.

Bromann, Jennifer. "Letting Go." *School Library Journal* 48, no. 7 (July 2002). Includes considerations for weeding your periodical collection.

Fine, Janna and Molly Kinney. "Magazine Mania." *School Library Journal* 46, no. 8 (August 2000). Includes a small list of magazines new in 2000. Due to the age of the article, about half the URLs did not work, but there are still some good listings.

Friedman, R. Seth. *Factsheet 5 Zine Reader.* (See also Web version: http://www.factsheet5.org.) A collection of writings from *Factsheet 5*, which was an online and print zine dedicated to reviewing zines. At one time, *Factsheet 5* was considered to be the most comprehensive zine review tool in existence. Unfortunately, this zine ceased publication in 1997, although there are rumors that it may return. This tool, published in 1997, archives a huge amount of information, but it may be quite out of date.

Jones, Patrick. *Connecting Young Adults and Libraries.* 2nd ed. New York: Neal-Schuman, 1999. This book has an annotated list of over 50 print magazines of interest to teens, including contact information for each title in the appendix. May be slightly dated.

Jones, Patrick and Joel Shoemaker. *Do It Right! Best Practices for Serving Young Adults in School and Public Libraries.* New York: Neal-Schuman, 2001. This book contains an annotated list of over 75 print titles.

Katz, Bill and Linda Sternberg Katz, eds. *Magazines for Libraries.* 11th ed. New Providence, NJ: Bowker, 2002. This is a continually revised reference tool that lists many print titles, including a good section of magazines for teenagers.

Nichols, Mary Anne. *Merchandising Library Materials to Young Adults.* Greenwood

Village, CO: Libraries Unlimited, 2002. Magazines are discussed throughout the book and there is also a section reviewing magazine shelving units.

Nichols, Mary Anne and C. Allen Nichols, eds. *Young Adults and Public Libraries.* Westport, CT: Greenwood Press, 1998. This book contains a chapter on magazines.

On-line Directories

You can explore magazines on the Internet through these directories:

Google Directory, http://directory.google.com. Google began as a Webcrawler and has evolved to include an Internet directory. Try the following paths:

> Kids and Teens > Teen Life > Magazines and E-zines
>
> Kids and Teens > Computers > Chats and Forums > Teens

Open Directory Project, http://www.dmoz.com. The Open directory Project is a selective, nonprofit Internet directory compiled and revised by volunteer "net-citizens" and editors. Try the following paths:

> Kids and Teens > Teen Life > Magazines and E-zines
>
> Kids and Teens > Teen Life > Chats and Forums
>
> Kids and Teens > Teen Life > Web Communities

Yahoo!, http://www.yahoo.com. Yahoo! is one of the most venerable Internet directories, having started in 1994. Yahoo! is actually an acronym for *Yet Another Hierarchical Officious Oracle*. Sites are listed by employees of Yahoo!, through their own search of the net and suggestions from users. Possible paths to try:

> Society and Culture > Magazines
>
> Society and Culture > Cultures and Groups > Teenagers > Magazines

Zeal, http://www.zeal.com. Zeal, owned by Looksmart.com, is a very selective Internet directory developed by the submissions of qualified volunteer members editors, called "Zealots." Check out the following paths:

> People & Chat > Forums & Lists > Communities Online > By Age Group > Teens
>
> Library > Society > News & Magazines > Magazines

Web Sites

Here are some valuable Web sites for researching teen magazines:

The Book of Zines: Readings from the Fringe, http://www.zinebook.com. An on-line directory of all things zine related, including a list of over 50 links to other zine directories. This portal can lead you to hundreds of zine reviews and links.

Invisible City Productions, http://www.invisible-city.com/zines/zinereviews.htm. Describes itself as a "collective of artists, writers, game designers, and zine editors, who provide this as a space for the creators of secret media to come together and touch antennae." Reviews several zines per season.

Los Angeles Public Library, http://www.lapl.org/teenscape/library/tsmagsub. html. List of over 150 teen magazines. Many of the magazine titles are links to their on-line counterparts, but beware: some links don't work.

Ohio Public Library Information Network, http://www.oplin.lib.oh.us. OH! Teens Page. Click on OH! Teens. Currently, this is a small selection, but it should grow. Follow this path: OH! Teens > Good Reads > E-Zines & Magazines.

Teen Reading, http://www.ala.org/yalsa. Page sponsored by the Young Adult Library Services Association (YALSA), a division of the American Library Association. There are many links, including one to "comics and zines," but relevant on-line tools can be found on all the pages. Follow this path: Electronic Resources > Teen Reading > Get Graphic @ your library.

YA Librarians' Homepage, http://yahelp.suffolk.lib.ny.us/yamags.html. List of over 30 titles, with links to on-line versions.

Zine World, http://www.undergroundpress.org/others.html. A Reader's Guide to the Underground Press. Resource for independent "underground" press. Has a listing of over 30 zine resources.

Topical List of Suggested Magazine Titles

Academic

Imagine, http://cty.jhu.edu/imagine/. Aimed at students who want to get more out of their education than school has to offer, *Imagine* offers reviews of extracurricular and summer programs. Sponsored by the Johns Hopkins University Center for Talented Youth.

Activism and Politics

Clamor, http://www.clamormagazine.org/. Produced by two twenty-some-things, this edgy alt-culture and politics magazine is best for older teens and adults.

Wire Tap, http://www.wiretapmag.org. The best on-line source for teen activism. Note: *Wire Tap* is on-line only—it has no print counterpart.

Anime, Manga, and Comics

Animerica, http://www.animerica-mag.com. This magazine features anime and manga reviews, fan art, and artist interviews.

Comics Journal, http://www.tcj.com. Investigates comics as an art form.

Games and Gaming

Computer Games Magazine, http://www.cgonline.com. The only independent computer gaming magazine, *CG* contains articles and game reviews.

GamePro, http://www.gamepro.com. The latest info on Playstation, Nintendo, Xbox, and PC games.

Alternative Lifestyle

XY, http://www.xy.com. A culture magazine for young gay men.

Girls

CosmoGirl!, http://www.cosmogirl.com. Fashion, advice, and articles for girls ages 15–24. A little bit hipper than *Seventeen*.

Sister 2 Sister, http://www.s2smagazine.com. A teen magazine aimed at African American girls.

Humor

Mad Magazine, http://www.madmag.com. The classic magazine, which features comics and parodies of pop culture.

The Onion, http://www.theonion.com. *The Onion* is a satire of traditional news-papers.

Literary

Teen Ink, http://www.teenink.com. This magazine consists entirely of writing by teen contributors, including fiction, poetry, college essays, and college re-views.

Music

Rolling Stone, http://www.rollingstone.com. News from the music industry as a
    whole. Generally geared toward adults, but teens read it as well.
SPIN, http://www.spin.com. Check out *SPIN* for news about and reviews of
    alternative music, heavy metal, imports—anything but pop.
Vibe, http://www.vibe.com. The most mainstream rap, hip-hop and R & B news
    and reviews.

Religious

Breakaway, http://www.family.org/teenguys/breakmag/. A Christian magazine
    for teen boys.
Brio, http://www.briomag.com. A Christian magazine for teen girls.

Sports

Sports Illustrated, http://www.sportsillustrated.com. The scoop on all the main-
    stream sports (basketball, baseball, football, and so on).
Thrasher, http://www.thrashermagazine.com. The magazine for skateboard cul-
    ture.
WWE, http://www.wwe.com/magazines/wwe/. World Wrestling Entertain-
    ment's official magazine.

Last Thoughts

Developing and maintaining a magazine collection is a great chance to
show teens that you're serious about what interests them, and that libraries
aren't just about books—that libraries can be as hip and dynamic as MTV.

2

BUT THOSE AREN'T REALLY BOOKS! GRAPHIC NOVELS AND COMIC BOOKS

David S. Serchay

Libraries have been dealing with comic books for over 60 years. Some have looked upon them favorably, while others have dismissed them as being inappropriate for a library setting. In recent years there has been increased interest in and acceptance of comics, and a greater interest in purchasing them for libraries. The purpose of this chapter is to tell you more about this "uniquely American art form" and its possible place in your library.

There are many reasons to develop a teen graphic novel and comic book collection. In this chapter, I will discuss those reasons, as well as other issues of importance as listed below:

- What are comic books, graphic novels, and trade paperbacks?
- Why should I buy them for my library?
- How do I buy them?
- What should I buy?
- Now that I have them, what should I do with them?

Comic books, graphic novels, and trade paperbacks (the last two will be referred to as graphic novels when discussed in general terms) come in various sizes and shapes, are presented in color or black and white, and cover a host of genres. Comics and graphic novels are often confused with each other, and you may ask, what is the difference between a graphic novel and a comic book? The main differences between the two forms are quality and length. Comic books average 48 pages or less, while graphic novels average 128 pages–plus (and cost between $8.99 and $24.99). Not to confuse things, but a bound collection of comic books can be described as a graphic novel.

While Superhero might be the most well-known genre in both formats, there are also comics and graphic novels that can fit into the following genres:

- Drama
- Adventure
- Romance
- Fantasy
- Science Fiction
- Horror
- History
- Current Events
- Crime
- Humor
- True-Life
- Science and Nature

Some of these are for all ages, while others are best for a more mature audience. Some are "quick reads," while others can take hours, if not days to get through. Remember—comics and graphic novels are a format, not a genre—while this may be arguable, for the purposes of this book, they are considered a format.

Long-Running Series

The longest-running American comic book series is Detective Comics, which began in 1937 (and introduced Batman two years later). However, due to various reasons, Action Comics, which introduced Superman in its 1938 premiere issue, has a higher number, which would normally indicate a longer "life span," but that is not the case in this instance.

COMIC BOOKS

While this chapter deals mainly with the more book-like graphic novels, you also might want to purchase individual comic books for your library. Comic books are to magazines as graphic novels are to books. Like magazines, they tend to be periodicals, printed on a much lighter paper than what is found in books. Information on the various types of comics follows.

Series

An ongoing title that is published on a regular—usually monthly—basis. They usually cost $2.00–$3.00, and are 32 pages (with ads); but both price and page count can be higher or lower. They have one or more stories, and those stories can be self-contained or continued in the next issue or in another title altogether. A series has an unknown life span. It could be canceled after a few months or run for decades. Series are also the only kind of comic to be sold by subscription.

Superheroes are the features in most of the better-known series titles, both in solo adventures and as parts of teams, with the more popular ones (Superman, Batman, Spider-Man, the X-Men) appearing in more than one title per month. For example, in a one-month period, the DC Comics character Batman might appear in *Batman: Detective Comics*, *Batman: Legends of the Dark Knight*, *Batman: Gotham Knights*, and the team book *LA*, and may appear in spin-off titles like *Robin* and *Batgirl*, plus *Batman Adventures*, which is inspired by the animated TV series.

Limited Series

Also called a mini- or maxi-series, a limited series has a predetermined number of issues, usually between 3 and 12. They can feature a character, who is the star of the series, or they might spotlight a secondary character, or feature a new character altogether. They may contain multiple stories and story lines, be one continuous story, or share a story with another series. They've also been used to "test the waters" of a character's popularity before launching that character into a series. On a few occasions, a title has continued as a series past the planned final issue, and on rare occasions, limited series have ended early.

While Batman is appearing in his monthly titles, he may be appearing in a limited series of adventures set early in his career (*Batman: The Long*

Halloween—1996–1997), or other current activities (*Batman: The Cult*—1988), teaming up with other characters (*Batman and Superman: World's Finest*—1999–2000), or even letting the focus fall on his supporting characters (*Batman: Gordon of Gotham*—1998). Some well-known limited series featuring characters without series of their own include *Watchmen* (DC Comics, 1986–1987) and the drama *Tale of One Bad Rat* (Dark Horse Comics, 1994–1995). A number of limited series are collected into trade paperbacks (see below).

Annuals

As the name implies, annuals come out on a yearly basis. Annuals are generally related to an existing series, although not always. A few annuals have been based on limited series or are published for characters who never got their own titles in any form. Annuals are usually two or three times as large as a standard comic book, and they may contain more than one story. In some years, a company's annuals will maintain a continuing storyline or have common themes.

Specials

Specials are an "extension" of the annual. These are similar in both size and format, but come out on an irregular basis, and may even contain the word "Special" in the title. Examples of a Special not referred to as such, are the *Secret Files* titles published by DC, which give additional background on characters. In some cases, there have been multiple issues printed, while others needed only one issue.

One-Shot

A title that is intended to be produced only once. Sometimes the one-shot will tie in to events that take place in another title, functioning as "supplemental material." On other occasions they've been used to present a character's adventures outside their own book. In recent years, one-shots have often been used to fill the occasional "fifth week" in the monthly release schedule, frequently containing a common theme such as "villains." They have also been used as parts of an ongoing story, with a two-issue limited series acting as "bookends." An example of this is *Sins of Youth* (2000), a DC Comics storyline in which teen heroes, who became adults and adult heroes, reverted to childhood in both appearance and personality. In between the publication of the two issues *Young Justice Sins of Youth* limited series, were eight one-shots, such as *Sins of Youth Batboy/Robin*.

Reprints

As the term implies, a reprint is a new printing of a previously published story or issue. Reprints appear as one-shots, as limited series, and even as ongoing titles. Sometimes they are released to help promote a related character and story line, or for a special event. The X-Men were featured in several ongoing reprint titles such as *X-Men Classic* (Marvel, 1986–1995) and in 2003 reprinted the 1980s Graphic Novel *God Loves, Man Kills* in comic book form (to tie into the X-Men movie sequel, which was partly inspired by that story). To celebrate the turn of the century, DC Comics published 52 *Millennium Edition* comics that were reprints from significant issues over the past 60+ years.

Digests

Referring more to size than anything, digests are square-bound books that are much smaller than a regular comic book. These are often found in places where regular comics are not, such as near a supermarket checkout counter next to the tabloids and *TV Guide*. For many years, *Archie Comics* have been produced in digest form, featuring reprints of stories from their series.

Something Unusual

Perhaps the oddest "extra" was in the 1997 collection of the 1985–86 Marvel Comics limited series *Squadron Supreme*. The writer, Mark Gruenwald, had died, and in his will he stated that he wanted to be cremated and "his ashes mixed in with the printer's ink during the printing process." As many, including Gruenwald, considered *Squadron Supreme* to be his best work, his ashes went into the trade paperback, which also contained tributes to him. This resulted in many black humor comments such as "I've heard of a writer throwing himself into his work but . . ." and "Who do we use if there's a second printing?" As it turns out, there was a second printing, but luckily for other creators it simply contains the words "Note: Second Printing Contains No Ashes."

Adaptations and Licensed Characters

While a number of comics have been made into TV shows and movies, the reverse is also true. Films and books have been fully adapted as comics (one of the best-known examples being *Classics Illustrated*). In many cases comics have presented new stories based on those characters. Popular licensed works include *Star Trek* and *Star Wars*, which have appeared as series, as limited series, as one-shots, and in other forms.

Manga

In Japan, comics—or Manga—are part of a $3 billion industry that accounts for as much as 60 percent of the printed materials sold there. Many popular titles have been translated and altered, since in Japan, the order of the pages, the arrangement of the panels, and even the order of the text in the word balloons is right to left. Therefore, the books must be "flopped" for American publication, though some companies have released some titles "unflopped," translated, but in the original order. Manga has been becoming more popular in America in recent years, due in part to the rising popularity of Japanese animation (anime). Some of the better-known titles include *Dragonball*, *Dragonball Z*, and *Ranma 1/2*.

Prestige Format

This is strictly a format, rather than a type of comic. Also called "Bookshelf Format," these comics are in square-bound form, with heavier paper stock, and are therefore able to be placed on a shelf with no problem. Both limited series and one-shots are released in this format, with the latter being preferable for library collections, as you won't have to worry about missing any series issues. The one-shots can even be processed and cataloged for your collection. One of the earliest books in this format was the classic *Batman: The Dark Knight Returns* (1986). Many of the prestige format limited series and one-shots published by DC Comics are *Elseworlds*, stories that put their characters into different times or settings, such as a Batman who fights Jack the Ripper.

GRAPHIC NOVELS

The term "graphic novel" has been defined as "a self-contained story that uses a combination of text and art to articulate the plot." In other words, authors use sequential art to tell the story. Many consider *A Contract With God* (1978), by Will Eisner, who is one of the true greats of the industry, to be the first graphic novel. Available in hard- or softcover, graphic novels are generally priced between $10.00 and $35.00, depending on size and format. Hardcover books are often reprinted with a lower-priced, softcover binding. They also come in a variety of shapes, including an oversized tabloid format.

Despite their name, you can sometimes find collections in hardcover, but usually for a higher price. Similar to the way DVDs contain added information and missing scenes, sometimes the trade paperback format will also include "extras," including forewords by noted authors, "behind the scenes" information, extra artwork, scripts, and even "missing scenes."

TRADE PAPERBACKS

While graphic novels almost always present original stories, trade paperbacks offer collections of reprinted comic book stories. Trade paperbacks often fit into at least one of four categories.

Collected Limited Series

When the issues of a limited series are collected into a single volume, the result is a collected limited series. Some comic readers prefer trade paperback versions to purchasing the individual issues, since the former fit easily on the bookshelf and the entire story can be read at once, instead of having to wait for up to a year for the conclusion.

Collected Story

This type of graphic novel presents multiple "chapters" of a connected story. While these chapters are often taken from a single title, this is not always the case. Sometimes, a story has crossed over into other series, one-shots, limited series, annuals, and elsewhere, and episodes may be drawn from these other sources.

Chronological Reprints

This type of trade paperback simply reprints a given number of issues of a particular comic book series, even if they are not part of the same story line. Often the next time a trade paperback for that series comes out, it starts on the issue in line (for example, if one collection contains issues 1–8, the next starts on issue 9). Sometimes a chronological reprint covers the same territory as a collected story; and on other occasions, a multipart story is included along with several stand-alone issues. Some reprint collections feature stories dating back to the 1930s and 1940s.

Theme

Stories with a common theme are featured in this type of trade paperback. Such a collection may feature different characters, different creators, or stories from different titles, some which span decades. For example, DC Comics has printed several trade paperbacks with the theme of "The Greatest Stories Ever Told," featuring stories about Batman, Superman, Team-Up, and so on. Marvel has published a number of theme trade paperbacks featuring the origins of their characters, often mixed with more contemporary tales.

WHY SHOULD I BUY COMIC BOOKS AND GRAPHIC NOVELS FOR MY LIBRARY?

If you're not asking this question, your superiors or patrons might well be. While public perception has improved over the years, some still see comics as "junk literature," fit only for little kids or people with poor reading skills. However, many graphic novels feature sophisticated language and story lines, and there are many solid reasons why graphic novels should be a part of your YA collection.

Educational Reasons

In the *Read Aloud Handbook*, Jim Trelease points out that "when a child reads a Tintin graphic novel, he is reading 8,000 words. The beautiful part is that children are unaware that they are reading 8,000 words."

Some might say it with derision, but some graphic novels appeal to and actually can benefit people with poor reading skills who are attempting to improve their abilities, or even your average reluctant reader. Studies have shown that significant amounts of light reading help encourage kids to read, leading to a lifetime habit of reading, and "a mastery of more difficult reading." Also, it has been demonstrated that students who regularly read comic books have better vocabularies and are more likely to read above their grade-level.

Comic book writer Scott McCloud, who also wrote the books *Understanding Comics* and *Reinventing Comics*, says that "Comics are a powerful tool for conveying the literary experience to a generation of readers comfortable with television and computers. There is a new visual literacy developing. Graphic Novels take advantage of this emerging literacy. The format also works well for reluctant readers who take more easily to titles that combine graphics with text."

And he provides a great reason for libraries to have graphic novels:

> The benefits of libraries collecting comics are the same benefits as reading comics. For children, comics have often been a doorway into literacy. But to see comics as only that is a mistake. Comics are a valid medium and can hold their own against the great works of traditional literature and can provide the same enrichments as prose and poetry. Certainly if libraries include video and sound collections, comics should also be included. Comics are probably closer to the mission statements of libraries than either of the previous two. And libraries can be in the forefront of educating the public that there's more to comics than guys in tights beating each other up. (McCloud 2000)

Reviewers Are Taking Note

Graphic novels have been gaining more and more mainstream recognition including:

- Reviews and articles in library publications such as *Library Journal*, *School Library Journal*, and *VOYA*, often on a regular basis.
- Reviews and articles in non-library publications like *The New York Times*, *Time*, and *Entertainment Weekly*.

Award Winners

The Harvey Awards

The Harvey Awards are one of the comics industry's oldest and most respected awards. The Harveys recognize outstanding achievements in 24 categories, ranging from Best Artist to the Jack Kirby Hall of Fame. They are the only industry awards both nominated by and selected by the full body of comics professionals.

The Eisners

The Eisners are named for the creator of *The Spirit* as well as such critically acclaimed graphic novels as *Contract With God* and *Family Matter*. These recognize the outstanding work of the creative people from within the comics' industry and help to attract public attention to the art form by publicizing to nonreaders the best work the industry has to offer.

In 1986, Art Spiegelman's *Maus* won the Pulitzer Prize. Using animals to represent people, the book is the story of his father's Holocaust experiences. A second Pulitzer Prize winner, Michael Chabon's novel *The Awesome Adventures of Kaviler and Clay* (2001), utilized the early days of comics as its subject.

The prestigious World Fantasy Award for best short story was awarded to Neil Gaiman and Charles Vess for #18 of the *Sandman* series, in which Shakespeare and company perform *A Midsummer Night's Dream* for the real Oberon and Titania. Soon thereafter, the rules were changed to prevent another comic book from receiving it again.

The comics field also has a number of its own awards, with the Harveys and the Eisners being among the most important.

Comics in Academia

Comics and graphic novels have been studied in college classrooms for years, mainly for literature classes, though for other subjects as well. High school curricula are even beginning to include these formats, with titles such as *Maus* appearing on required reading lists. Academic libraries, especially those with strong popular culture collections, include comic books and graphic novels in their collections. "Comic Books and Graphic Novels in School and Public Libraries" is even taught as a course at the American Library Association–accredited School of Library and Information Studies at the University of Alberta.

Films and Television

In recent years, a number of films and television shows based on comics and graphic novels have been released. They include superhero titles as well as other genres. Some examples follow:

- Daredevil (2003)—Marvel Comics–based film
- X-Men (2000)—Marvel Comics–based film
- Spider-Man (2002)—Marvel Comics–based film
- Hulk (2003)—Marvel Comics–based film
- From Hell (2001)—Graphic novel–based film
- The Road to Perdition (2002)—Graphic novel–based film
- Ghost World (2001)—Graphic novel–based film
- Smallville (2001–present)—DC Comics–based television program
- Birds of Prey (2002–present)—DC Comics–based television program

Many of these films and television shows have been highly successful with the public, and with critics as well. They feature major, and often award-winning, performers such as Tom Hanks, Halle Berry, Thora Birch, Kirsten Dunst, Johnny Depp, and Ian McKellen. The popularity of these films and programs expands interest in the library's Graphic Novels collection, the same way a film based on a novel increases that title's popularity.

Comic Writers in Other Mediums

Many comic books have become the basis of novels, both through adaptations and through original stories. For example, novels have been published that feature Batman, Spider-Man, The Hulk, and other superheroes. In addition, novelizations of comic book stories such as the 1992 *Death of Superman* and the 1996 limited series *Kingdom Come* have been done. In the latter cases, these works are expanded upon in novel form, much as the novelization of a movie expands on the original work. There are also several comic book writers who have written their own novels and have even worked in TV and film. They include Peter David, Chris Claremont, and Neil Gaiman.

Some novelists and television and movie writers write comics too. These include:

- J. Michael Straczynski (Babylon 5)
- Joss Whedon (Buffy the Vampire Slayer)
- Kevin Smith (Chasing Amy, Dogma)
- Brad Meltzer (*New York Times* best-selling author)

Popularity in Other Libraries

Libraries around the country have been discovering Graphic Novels, at times establishing large collections. In 1999, GNLIB-L, an on-line mailing list dedicated to the topic, was founded (see below for more information). In 2002, the Young Adult Library Services Association (YALSA) hosted a day-long preconference, "Getting Graphic @ Your Library" at the American Library Association (ALA) Annual Conference, and it turned out to be the highest attended preconference that year. "Getting Graphic @ Your Library" was also the theme of Teen Read Week that year. And that leads us into the next reason ...

Increased Circulation

The popularity of graphic novels has led to increased circulation in libraries that carry them. Neil Gaiman has told of the experience of British libraries when they began to stock graphic novels. Those libraries noticed that they were constantly being checked out, and were bringing in new readers as well. The presence of comics in one junior high school library resulted in an 82 percent increase in library traffic and a 30 percent increase in the circulation of non-comic books. It is estimated that five million people purchase comic books each year, and teens have identified graphic novels as one of their preferred reading formats.

Graphic novels can even be used as a way to increase the circulation of other books. If a teen has enjoyed a graphic novel in the adventure, fantasy, or science fiction genre, then you can lead them to similar themed novels.

Four Reasons to Collect Graphic Novels and Trade Paperbacks

Stephen Weiner, author of *100 Graphic Novels for Libraries* and *The 101 Best Graphic Novels*, gives these reasons to collect graphic novels and trade paperbacks:

- to strengthen the collection by adding works of cultural value,
- to encourage new patrons by adding a medium they enjoy to the collection,
- to renew regular patrons by adding new types of mediums to the collections,
- to support and nurture artistic works in the comics medium.

Below you will find the responses from a group of (primarily youth services) librarians when they were surveyed on the GN-LIB mailing list. The group was asked about the popularity of graphic novels in their libraries.

- "Since day one all have been going out at an alarming rate. I haven't seen *Star Wars: Dark Empire* on the shelves since it was cataloged. The popular titles are circulating 2–3 times a month [and] it would be more if they were returned quicker."—Brad Honigford, YA Specialist, Putnam County District Library, Ottawa, OH.

- "I can't keep them on the shelf!!! Generally, I only have about six or eight titles (out of 30) in the library at any one time."—Kimberly Paone, Teen Services Librarian, Elizabeth Public Library, Elizabeth, NJ.

- "They seem more in demand than other genres—that's mostly due to the small group of readers who are devoted to graphic novels and are willing to ask for stuff, place holds on stuff, bug us until it gets in, etc. etc. Not much else inspires that behavior."—Sarah Dentan, Teen Services Librarian, Berkeley Public Library, West Branch, Berkeley, CA.

- "HOT HOT HOT—by far the best circulating thing in my collection. YA circulation has zoomed between 25 and 50 percent monthly."—Lesley Knieriem, former Young Adult Librarian, South Huntington Public Library, Long Island, NY.

- "With very little marketing, the graphic novels are circulating healthily. I have overheard word-of-mouth recommendations."— Jane Acheson, Children's Librarian, Norwell Public Library, Norwell, MA.

Now one cannot be sure whether all of the circulation is from teens or if some of it is from adults, but the popularity of the genre is definitely apparent.

A final reason comes from librarian Jane Halsell of the McHenry Public Library District, who said on GN-LIB that "the very best reason to collect graphic novels is that they are good books—some of them are extraordinary."

PURCHASING—THE HOW, WHICH, AND WHAT

When purchasing graphic novels for your library, you will probably use the same vendors that you use for regular purchases. Book Wholesalers Inc. and Ingram are among those vendors who have been promoting their graphic novel titles. However, many who have set up graphic novel collections use additional sources as well, including bookstores and on-line sources. The most popular alternative is the local comic book store.

Comics were once sold on newsstands along with magazines, but starting in the 1960s, shops began to open where comics were the main, or at least a major, focus. While there are fewer shops than there once were, these stores remain a great place for the librarian to not only purchase materials (you might even be able to arrange a discount), but also learn additional information about the genre. Who better than someone who sells comics and graphic novels to teens to let you know what titles teens are interested in?

One advantage of purchasing from a vendor is that you can reinforce the binding. Many graphic novels have soft covers, and by going through a vendor you can use the vinabind process to reinforce it, or even use the more expensive pre-binding process, which turns a paperback into a hardcover. These processes can help to extend the "shelf-life" of the book. But don't forget to consider what is likely to meet the needs of your particular teens in making this decision.

Diamond

Like libraries, comic book shops receive their materials from distributors instead of from publishers. The biggest distributor is Diamond. Libraries can deal directly with Diamond. This distributor prints a monthly catalog called *Previews* that contains a list of everything that will be released that month (including comics-related paraphernalia such as books, toys, and posters). Not only does *Previews* show that month's releases, but major companies also maintain a backlist of older titles, mainly for graphic novels and trade paperbacks. Remember that *Previews* is created for promotional purposes, and thus it shouldn't be used as a source of reviews.

Founded in 1982, Diamond is the world's largest distributor of English-language comic books, graphic novels, and comics-related merchandise. While they deal mainly with retailers, they have also worked with schools, literacy programs, and libraries. Their catalog, which can be ordered by calling 1-800-452-6642, and their on-line catalog found at http://bookshelf.diamondcomics.com/ contain a large number of graphic novels and trade paperbacks, as well as some comics-related fiction and nonfiction works. The titles are divided into recommended ages (children, YA, and adult), and are also divided into categories such as fantasy, action/adventure, humor, and literature. Cataloging and subject heading suggestions are also given, and the Web page includes reviews and even lesson plans. While there are many titles not listed and while you may use other vendors for the actual purchasing, the Diamond catalog and Web page are good sources of information.

Publishers

There are about 50 regular publishers of comics, together producing hundreds of comics each month. Some release dozens each month, while others publish only one or two. Here is information on some of them.

DC Comics

This is the largest publishing company and the publisher of the adventures of Superman, Batman, and Wonder Woman, as well as other well-known superhero characters. During the 1980s, DC began publishing titles meant for mature audiences, such as the 1986 limited series *Watchmen*, and eventually, thanks in part to *Sandman*, creating the mature audience based Vertigo line of titles in the 1990s (the level of "maturity" ranges from PG-13 to R). DC also publishes books aimed at younger children.

Marvel Comics

Marvel Comics is the other half of what has been called "The Big Two." Marvel prints a large number of books each month including several *Spider-Man* titles and *X-Men* spin-offs. Other popular titles include *The Incredible Hulk*, *The Fantastic Four*, and *The Avengers*. They have recently established the "Max" line of mature-audience comics.

Dark Horse

Dark Horse has become one of the biggest of what is now known as the "Independent" publishers. Besides a number of original titles, such as *Hellboy*, Dark Horse comics produces a number of comics based on other media such as the *Star Wars* films and *Buffy the Vampire Slayer*. It is also one of the major distributors of Manga, translated for English-speaking audiences.

Image

Image was founded by a number of comics professionals in the early 1990s and has several creator-owned imprints, with perhaps the most successful titles being *Spawn* from Todd McFarlane Productions and *Witchblade* from Top Cow. One Image imprint, Wildstorm, is now part of DC Comics.

Archie

Since the 1940s Archie has been publishing the adventures of teenager Archie Andrews and his friends in the town of Riverdale.

Bongo

Bongo's titles include those based on the popular television show *The Simpsons*.

Viz

Viz is the largest publisher of Manga in America.

Crossgen

This Florida-based company publishes work of fantasy, science fiction, adventure, and mystery.

Publisher Cooperation

On occasion, characters from two companies have been paired together. DC's Batman has teamed with Marvel's Captain America and Image's Spawn, and has fought two of Dark Horse's "licensed properties," Aliens and Predator. DC and Marvel's heroes even fought each other in a 1996-limited series.

Some of the other publishers you may want to look for include Oni, Fantagraphics, Tokyopop, Top Shelf, Drawn & Quarterly, and Cartoon Books. Web sites for these and other companies can be found at the end of the chapter.

Professional Resources

Print Versions

There are a number of publications that discuss and review comics and graphic novels, including *Comic Shop News*, *Comic Buyers Guide*, and *Wizard*. Many libraries purchase these for their YA area. *The Comics Journal* takes a more critical look at the genre.

Web Sites

There are also many Web sites dealing with comics and graphic novels, several of which are created by librarians, including "Recommended Graphic Novels for Public Libraries," "Comic Book for Young Adults," "Librarian's Guide to Anime and Manga," and "The Comics Get Serious," which has been created by D. Aviva Rothschild, the author of *Graphic Novels: A Bibliographic Guide to Book-Length Comics* (Libraries Unlimited, 1995). Please refer to the list at the end of the chapter for addresses and additional Web sites.

Mailing Lists and Listservs

Many of the library mailing lists including PUBYAC, YA-YAAC, and YALSA-BK, have occasional discussions on graphic novels, but for the most and best information on graphic novels, the place to go is GNLIB-L. Founded in 1999, it has over 200 members, including writers of books on comics, creators of comic Web sites, representatives from library distributors and comic companies, people who work in comic shops, and, of course, librarians from all over, many of whom work with teens. The GNLIB Web site resides at http://www.angelfire.com/comics/gnlib. It includes access information, archives of old postings, suggested Web sites, and more. The list provides a multitude of suggestions for what to buy, program suggestions, and more. This is THE place for information on Graphic Novels in libraries (information on joining the list can be found at the end of the chapter).

Personal Judgment

Of course, even with all of the places to look for recommendations, the best and final judge is yourself. You know what will work in your library and what will not. You know your community, patrons, and collection. What's best for one branch in a multibranch library system might not be good for another. What can be easily placed in a public library might be problematic for a school library. Graphic novels may be in a different format, but you should evaluate them using the same criteria as you would anything else that you buy for your collection.

The best way to evaluate a title is to examine it yourself. Then you can form an opinion of the story and art quality and whether the content is appropriate. Following are some suggestions for doing this.

Using the Local Comic Shop

Develop a relationship with the shop owner/manager of your local comic shop. Most shops won't have a place to do any "in-depth" reading of the material, and in fact often discourage it. Additionally, many shops will put the books into taped-up plastic bags (some hardcover editions come in shrink-wrapped plastic). If you have a relationship with the shop's staff, they might let you take comics out of the bags and read them there.

Local Bookstores

A bookstore can also be a good place for evaluations, especially some of the larger chain stores, which have no problem with people sitting around and reading. Some stores even have special sections for graphic novels. Others tend to place them in or near their Science Fiction/Fantasy or Humor sections.

Interlibrary Loan (ILL)

With so many libraries purchasing graphic novels, it is very easy to use WorldCat to seek titles from outside your library system. If you do not have WorldCat access, there are a few other ways to ILL books (check with your library for its standard methods). While a book might take longer to find, you are also able to take it home for a longer evaluation period or even share it with coworkers or a teen advisory board. Using ILL will also provide information on how other libraries are treating graphic novels in terms of binding and cataloging.

It does not matter which method you use; previewing before purchasing is much more preferable than buying a title first, and then finding that it is totally unsuitable for your collection. At the end of the chapter you'll find a list of suggested titles and a list of books, along with Web sites for additional suggestions.

CATALOGING

Once you've decided what you want to purchase for your collection, the next question is "where are you going to put it?" Depending on your library this might be your decision, or it might be a decision made by others who allow you only to make suggestions. How a graphic novel is cataloged and where it is shelved will have an impact on how easy or difficult it will be for a patron to find the book. In most of these cases the proper age-related prefixes, such as "J," "YA," or "Teen," are added when necessary. When it comes to cataloging, some of the more popular methods include the ideas listed below.

Dewey Number

Most libraries tend to put comics and graphic novels in the 741.59 area, with some "non-fiction" titles being placed elsewhere (*Maus*, for example, is often shelved with other books on the Holocaust). Libraries using Library of Congress designations tend to use PN 6728 (or thereabout).

The method of separating nonfiction from fiction graphic novels can pose difficulties for teen readers. Teens will need to search for "their" title among other "boring" nonfiction works. This is often perceived as a barrier, especially by reluctant readers. If this method is chosen, it would be best to "segregate" the graphic novels in a separate display, shelving range, etc. while still utilizing Dewey or LC order. Segregating the collection also assists browsers.

Fiction

These are cataloged the same way as "regular" fiction titles, by author (or primary author), or by title in the case of an anthology. This method can also be challenging for teens, and again, it doesn't promote browsing.

Special Designation

Some libraries assign graphic novels a catalog "number" of "graphic novel," "GN," or "Comix" or other special listings. For example, in the card/computer catalog the listing might be "GN Fic Gaiman."

WEEDING

When it comes to replacing and/or weeding graphic novels from the collection, again, treat them as you would any other books. Are they worth replacing? Are they circulating? If your graphic novel collection in general has very little circulation, you might want to consider publicizing them or moving them to a more prominent spot before removing them.

SHELVING

When it comes to shelving, certain issues must be considered. First and foremost, graphic novels should be in the library's teen collection. This will allow for the easiest access for the collection's target audience.

- Do you have a separate young adult or teen collection?
- Are your graphic novels in 741.59 or nonfiction areas? If so, is your library's juvenile, teen, and adult nonfiction separate or interfiled?
- Are you planning to put the graphic novels in a special place in the library?
- What age range do you consider Young Adult? If your young adult collection is aimed at students 12–15, then you may need to more carefully examine the wide-ranging subjects and appropriateness of certain titles.
- Who is allowed in the adult and young adult sections?

INTELLECTUAL FREEDOM ISSUES

If you have a special section for graphic novels, or if they are in a separate children's/YA area, then it is easier to make sure that age-appropriate material is placed there. With a mixed collection, there is a risk that a teen, or in a more problematic situation, a child, might find a book meant for adults (containing language and nudity), while looking for something more "innocent." This can lead to complaints from parents, or from those who feel that all comics are meant for children. If you do have a separate area for graphic novels, make sure that shelvers know about it, and that they don't put the more mature titles in the children's area.

The question of what to do with the so-called "mature audience titles" is one which you will have to decide for yourselves, often on a book-by-book basis. Sometimes these titles can be tame, while others are definitely meant for adults. A possible problem with mature audience graphic novels is that they are "visual," and while a YA novel may describe a scene that some might find objectionable, the graphic novel illustrates it as well.

Foreign works should also be considered. In Japan, nudity is not taboo as it is in America. Because of this, nudity appears in some manga aimed at a teen audience. This nudity is often nonsexual in nature and is used to show bathing or for comic effect. For example, one of the most popular Manga series in America is *Ranma 1/2* by Rumiko Takahashi, one of the world's most popular female comic artists. It is a story about a teenage boy who turns into a busty, red-headed girl when splashed with cold water. So, on several occasions, a topless boy becomes a topless girl.

Sandman presents an interesting case as well. It is a critically acclaimed series that incorporates elements of fantasy, religion, history, mythology, and literature. It also has, in various issues, sex, violence, nudity, alternate sexuality, and story lines about which some may object. The Sandman books are highly recommended, almost a "must have" for any collection, but it is up to the individual library if it is to be purchased, and if so, if it should be cataloged as YA or Adult.

Some publishers identify their books as for "mature audience[s]." This provides another reason why you should try to read the book, or have it reviewed, prior to purchase, even though in most cases it is not difficult to "reclassify" the book "up" or "down" if needed. Also, talk to the person who orders the adult titles in your library. If that person can purchase the "mature" titles and place them in the adult section, it may simplify the decision for you. If your library has no age restrictions, a teen can still have access, and, in case of complaints, you have the defense that it was placed in an older area.

Will mature audience material cause complaints? Perhaps, though so might titles aimed for a younger age. There might be complaints about the "visuals," such as the way a female character might be drawn or clothed. There might be complaints about the story itself, much as there may be complaints about the content of "text" books. One librarian reported that a parent complained because a Batman story featured a prostitute. Complaints should, of course, be handled the same way as complaints for any other materials.

THEFT AND SECURITY ISSUES

Because graphic novels are so popular, an added concern is theft, a concern shared with all other library materials. Comics' writer and editor Mike Gold said that when he was editor of the *Classics Illustrated* line of comics, he was told by a number of school administrators that they did not purchase comics for their libraries because "they don't walk off the shelf, they run." While this may be the case in some libraries, the GN-LIB surveys show that the percentage of graphic novels missing was no greater than for any other popular subject. They found those that were lost/not returned to be less of a problem than the books falling apart after much use.

Of course, you can take additional precautions to help defer theft, besides the usual methods. These might include stamping the materials and even defacing them or cracking the spine. This at least will lessen its temptation as a "collector's" item, since the thief would have a greater difficulty in selling a "damaged" book.

PROGRAMMING, PROMOTION, AND OUTREACH

If you are purchasing a "starter collection" of graphic novels for your library, or even just increasing the number of books, you can use this as an opportunity for programming. A "comic book day" at the library, in which you tell teens about the collection, is one example. If there is a nearby comic shop, consider asking them for items to give out or raffle (many shops have a bin of cheap back issues).

Don't Have Time for Programming?

There are many ways to promote your collection if you don't have time to program or are just not interested. They include:

- Displays in the Library
- Posters and Bookmarks (ALA has superhero-related ones)
- Press Releases
- Giveaways (check with your local comic shop for "freebees" or cheap comic books to give as prizes).

The more artistic among you can even try a "comic book making" workshop, in which you demonstrate how a comic book is created. Books such as *The DC Comics Guide to Writing Comics* by Dennis O'Neil and *The DC Comics Guide to Penciling Comics* by Klaus Janson can be helpful for these programs. Or perhaps there's some local talent in your area, who would be willing to share their expertise for a nominal fee.

If you're lucky and have the funding, the best possible program for your library would be to have a professional comic writer/illustrator as a guest. You can get contact information from publishers, and many of these professionals are on-line. You may even have one in your area and not even know it. How much the pro would charge is, of course, up to them.

Finally, you can use outreach programs to promote the collection. When you visit schools for booktalks, take some graphic novels with you. They will help to interest the kids into coming to the library, and once there, you can show them everything else in your collection.

In 60 years, our profession has gone from articles in library publications warning of the "dangers" of comics to graphic novels being the theme of Teen Read Week. The relationship between comics and libraries continues to grow, and with this growth will come even more opportunity to attract teenagers into your library.

ADDITIONAL READINGS

Reviewing Sources

Library Journal and *VOYA* review graphic novels on a regular basis. Other related publications, such as *School Library Journal* and *Booklist*, also occasionally carry reviews. *Entertainment Weekly* is one of the better-known non-library publications that will occasionally review graphic novels. Also, there are the comic-related publications *Wizard* (http://www.wizard universe.com), *Comics Buyer's Guide* (http://www.collect.com/comics/), and *The Comics Journal* (http://www.tcj.com/).

I owe a special thanks to Stephen Weiner, Steve Miller, Gail de Vos, Hillary Chang, and the members of GN-LIB, especially Brad Honigford, Kimberly Paone, Sarah Dentan, Lesley Knieriem, Jane Acheson, Jane Halsell, Mike Pawuk, Rosemarie Grainer, Mari Hardacre, Blair Christolon, Stephen Raiteri, Patricia Foster, and Beth Gallaway.

For additional suggestions beyond the information in this chapter, look through the following books:

These two books cover titles for all ages, but can offer some good suggestions for a teen collection.

Rothschild, D. Aviva. *Graphic Novels: A Bibliographic Guide to Book-Length Comics.* Englewood, CO: Libraries Unlimited, 1995.

Weiner, Stephen. *The 101 Best Graphic Novels.* New York: NBM, 2001. There are several versions of this book. ISBN: 1–56163–285–6 is the "librarians" edition, which includes the supplement *Starting & Maintaining a Graphic Novel Collection* with a foreword by Neil Gaiman.

And for more books on comics and comics history:

Eisner, Will. *Comics & Sequential Art.* Tamarac, FL: Poorhouse Press, 1985. One of the best books on the subject by one of its greatest men, this book explains how comic art tells a story.

Flowers, James R. Jr. *The Incredible Internet Guide to Comic Books and Superheroes.* Tempe, AZ: Facts on Demand Press, 2000. The Internet has expanded comics' fan base to a higher level. This book provides information on what is available on the Web.

Goulart, Ron. *Comic Book Culture: An Illustrated History*. Portland, OR: Collector's Press, 2000.

Harvey, Robert C. *The Art of the Comic Book*. Jackson: University Press of Mississippi, 1996.

Hegenberger, John. *Collector's Guide to Comic Books*. Radnor, PA: Wallace-Homestead Books, 1990.

McCloud, Scott. *Reinventing Comics*. New York: HarperCollins, 2000.

————. *Understanding Comics*. New York: HarperCollins, 1994. These two works by McCloud examine the past, present, and future of comics.

Nyberg, Amy Kiste. *Seal of Approval: The History of the Comics Code*. Jackson: University Press of Mississippi, 1998. Discusses attempts to regulate and censor the contents of comic books over the years, including congressional hearings and the establishment of the Comics Code in the 1950s.

Owens, Thomas S. *Collecting Comic Books: A Young Person's Guide*. Brookfield, CT: Millbrook Press, 1995. A good guide on comics collection, aimed at elementary school–aged collectors.

Robbins, Trina. *From Girls to Grrrlz: A History of (WOMEN) Comics From Teens to Zines*. San Francisco: Chronicle Books, 1999. Examines the roles of female characters in comics over the years.

Sabin, Roger. *Comics, Comix, & Graphic Novels: A History of Comic Art*. London: Phaidon Press Ltd., 1996.

Schodt, Frederik L. *Manga! Manga! The World of Japanese Comics*. Tokyo, Japan: Kodansha International LTD, 1983, 1997. Over the past 15 years, Manga has become more and more popular in America. This book examines the phenomenon.

Wright, Nicky. *The Classic Era of American Comics*. Lincolnwood, IL: Contemporary Books, 2000.

SUGGESTED WEB SITES TO REVIEW

Comic Book Companies

AiT/PlanetLar, http://www.ait-planetlar.com.

Alternative Comics, http://www.indyworld.com/altcomics.

Archie, http://www.archie.com.

Bongo, http://www.littlegreenman.com.

Cartoon Books, http://www.boneville.com.

CrossGeneration (aka Crossgen), http://www.crossgen.com.

DC, http://www.dccomics.com.

Dark Horse, http://www.darkhorse.com.

Fantagraphics, http://www.fantagraphics.com.

Humanoids, http://www.humanoids-publishing.com.

Image, http://www.imagecomics.com.

Marvel, http://www.marvel.com.

NBM, http://www.nbmpub.com.

Oni, http://www.onipress.com.

Slave Labor, http://www.slavelabor.com.

TokyoPop, http://www.tokyopop.com.

Top Shelf, http://www.topshelfcomix.com.

Viz, http://www.viz.com.

Sources for Purchasing Comic Books and Graphic Novels

Amazon, http://www.amazon.com.

Book Wholesalers, Inc., http://www.bwibooks.com (free registration required).

Diamond Comics (main), http://www.diamondcomics.com; (library page), http://bookshelf.diamondcomics.com/.

The Master List of Comic Book & Trading Card Stores, http://www.the-master-list.com/.

The New Comic Book Releases List, http://www.comiclist.com.

Third Planet Comics and Games, http://www.graphicnovels.com.

News, Reviews, and Recommendations

Comic Book Resources, http://www.comicbookresources.com/.

Comic Books For Young Adults, http://ublib.buffalo.edu/libraries/units/lml/comics/pages.

Comics Continuum, http://www.comicscontinuum.com.

The Comics Get Serious, http://www.rationalmagic.com/Comics/Comics.html.

The Comics Journal, http://www.tcj.com.

Comics Worth Reading, http://www.comicsworthreading.com.

No Flying, No Tights: A Website Reviewing Graphic Novels for Teens, http://www.noflyingnotights.com.

Pulse: Comic Book News, Opinion & Insight, http://www.comicon.com/pulse.

Recommended Graphic Novels for Public Libraries, http://my.voyager.net/~sraiteri/graphicnovels.htm.

Sequential Tart, http://www.sequentialtart.com/home.shtml.

E-Mail Lists

GNLIB-L: A listserv for Young Adult and Adult Librarians, dealing with the subject of Graphic Novels in libraries. To subscribe, send a blank e-mail to GNLIB-L-subscribe@topica.com. To read the archive from this listserv, go to http://www.topica.com/lists/GNLIB-L and click on "Read this List." The official GNLIB-L Web site is http://www.angelfire.com/comics/gnlib.

PUBYAC: The list covers the practical aspects of Children and Young Adult Services in Public Libraries. To join the list and receive the mailings from PUBYAC, send a message to listproc@prairienet.org. No subject is necessary, and for the message type "subscribe pubyac."

YA-YAAC: To allow teen library advisory groups and the librarians who coordinate them in school and public libraries to share information and ideas. All those groups with e-mail addresses or fax numbers that are included in the National Youth Participation Database are subscribers of YA-YAAC. The YALSA Youth Participation Committee is also included. To subscribe send a message to listproc@ala.org. Leave the subject line blank. For the message type "Subscribe YA-YAAC first name last name."

YALSA-BK: An open list for book discussion. Subscribers are invited to discuss specific titles, as well as other issues concerning young adult reading and young adult literature. Send an e-mail message to listproc@ala.org. Leave the subject line blank. In the body of the message, type "Subscribe YALSA-bk your first name last name."

Usenet

Usenet has long been a place for discussion on comics and graphic novels. Message posters include fans, amateur and professional reviewers, and even comics pros. If you cannot access Usenet through other means, use the Google groups search engine at http://www.google.com (select "Groups" from the home page).

Some of the more popular Usenet Comics groups are:

- rec.arts.comics.dc.universe
- rec.arts.comics.marvel.universe
- rec.arts.comics.marvel.xbooks
- rec.arts.comics.misc

COMIC BOOK AND GRAPHIC NOVEL RECOMMENDATIONS

There are a great many titles out there to choose from, and many different lists for recommendations. (Some of these can be found in the books and Web sites mentioned in this chapter.)

In 2002, YALSA published a list of its top 25 graphic novels for teens (see box). For this chapter, I am including a list of some of the titles I feel should be among the titles you should include when establishing a graphic novel collection. These cover a number of genres. Superhero is the best-known genre, but a mix of genres can enhance your collection. These titles are also age-appropriate for teenagers, but some are intended for older teens and will be indicated as such.

Batman—There are over 75 Batman-related books available, ranging from "prestige format" one-shot to Trade Paperbacks to original graphic novels. Some are even "Elseworlds," which put Batman into other times and places such as Camelot or the Civil War. Notable books include:

> *Batman: Black and White* by Various Authors—DC Comics. A collection of various short stories by a number of popular writers and artists.
>
> *Batman: The Dark Knight Returns (Tenth Anniversary Edition)* by Frank Miller—DC Comics, ISBN: 1–56389–342–8, $14.95. Batman must bring himself out of retirement, in this first prestige format title, to fight both new and old threats. Includes a preliminary script treatment for the last part.

The graphic novels listed below were selected as notable by YALSA's 2002 Popular Paperbacks Committee. A complete list of the nominations can be found at http:/www.ala.org/yalsa/booklists/poppaper/02popapernoms. html.

Bendis, Brian-Michael—*Ultimate Spider-Man: Power and Responsibility*

Brennan, Michael—*Electric Girl*

Busiek, Kurt—*Kurt Busiek's Astro City: Life in the Big City*

Clowes, Daniel—*Ghost World*

Dixon, Chuck and Jordan Gorfinkel—*Birds of Prey*

Fujishima, Kosuke—*Oh My Goddess! 1-555-GODDESS*

Gaiman, Neil—*Death: The High Cost of Living*

Groening, Matt—*Bart Simpson's Treehouse of Horror Spine-Tingling Spooktacular*

Hosler, Jay—*Clan Apis*

Kudo, Kazuya—*Mai the Psychic Girl*

Loeb, Jeph—*Batman: The Long Halloween*

Medley, Linda—*Castle Waiting Lucky Road*

Millar, Mark—*Ultimate X-Men: The Tomorrow People*

Miyazaki, Hayao—*Nausicaa of the Valley of Wind Perfect Collection Vol. 1*

Moore, Alan—*Promethea Book One*

Moore, Terry—*Strangers in Paradise High School!*

Nishiyama, Yuriko—*Harlem Beat No. 1*

Petrie, Doug—*Buffy the Vampire Slayer: Ring of Fire*

Sakai, Stan—*Usagi Yojimbo: Grasscutter*

Smith, Jeff—*Bone Out from Boneville*

Smith, Kevin—*Daredevil Visionaries*

Takahashi, Rumiko—*Ranma 1/2 Volume 1*

Watson, Andi—*Geisha*

Winick, Judd—*Pedro & Me: Friendship, Loss, & What I Learned*

Winick, Judd—*The Adventures of Barry Ween, Boy Genius*

Batman: The Long Halloween by Jeph Loeb and Tim Sale—DC Comics, ISBN: 1–56389–469–6, $12.95. Early in his career, Batman must deal with a serial killer who kills on the holidays, a brewing mob war, and a host of villains, one of whom used to be his best friend.

Bone—Popular fantasy series by Jeff Smith, dealing with the adventures of the three Bone cousins, Fone, Phoney, and Smiley. The comic books have been collected in the following volumes from Cartoon Books and are available in both hard (HC) and softcover (SC).

Bone, Vol. 1: Out From Boneville, ISBN: 0–96366–099–3, $19.95 (HC); ISBN: 0–96366–094–2, $12.95 (SC).

Bone, Vol. 2: The Great Cow Race, ISBN: 0–96366–098–5, $22.95 (HC); ISBN: 0–96366–095–0, $12.95 (SC).

Bone, Vol. 3: Eyes of the Storm, ISBN: 0–96366–097–7, $24.95 (HC); ISBN: 0–96366–096–9, $16.95 (SC).

Bone, Vol. 4: The Dragonslayer, ISBN: 1–88896–301–8, $24.95 (HC); ISBN: 1–88896–300–X, $16.95 (SC).

Bone, Vol. 5: Rock Jaw, Master of the Eastern Border, ISBN: 1–88896–302–6, $22.95 (HC); ISBN: 1–88896–303–4, $14.95 (SC).

Bone, Vol. 6: Old Man's Cave, ISBN: 1-88896-304-2, $23.95 (HC); ISBN: 1–88896–305–0, $15.95 (SC).

Bone, Vol. 7: Ghost Circles, ISBN: 1–88896–308–5, $24.95 (HC); ISBN: 1-88896-309-3, $16.95 (SC).

Bone, Vol. 8: Treasure Hunters, ISBN: 1–88896–312–3, $23.95 (HC); ISBN: 1-88896-313-1, $15.95 (SC).

There are also these companion volumes:

Rose (with art by Charles Vess), ISBN: 1–88896–310–7, $29.95 (HC).

Stupid, Stupid Rat Tales (cowritten by Tom Sniegoski, with art by Stan Sakai), ISBN: 1–88896–306–9, $9.95 (SC).

Books of Magic by Neil Gaiman—DC Comics, ISBN: 1–56389–082–8, $19.95. The *other* British boy who becomes a wizard and has an owl. Tim Hunter is shown the magic worlds of the DC Universe. The resulting comic book series has been collected into several volumes.

Camelot 3000 by Mike W. Barr and Brian Bolland—DC Comics, ISBN: 0–930–28930–7, $14.95. King Arthur is awakened in the year 3000 to stop an alien invasion. Along with Merlin, the reincarnated Knights of the Round Table, and a man of that era, Arthur must protect England and earth not only from the Aliens, but from the workings of the evil Morgan LeFay.

Clan Apis by Jay Hosler—Active Synapse, ISBN: 0–967–72550–X, $15.00. This graphic novel about the life of bees, both provides an entertaining story and teaches the reader a little of the insect world.

Concrete—The adventures of a man who has been placed into a stone body by aliens. He now makes a living doing jobs that others cannot. These are authored by Paul Chadwick and are published by Dark Horse Comics.

Complete Concrete, ISBN: 1–56971–037–6, $24.95 (HC).

Think Like a Mountain, ISBN: 1–56971–176–3, $17.95 (SC).

Fax From Sarajevo by Joe Kubert—Dark Horse Comics, ISBN: 1–56971–346–4, $16.95. This award-winning graphic novel by comics legend Joe Kubert tells the true story of his friend Ervin Rustemagic, who lived with his family in Sarajevo during the city's 18-month siege from 1992 to 1993. Ervin's only link to his friends in the outside world was a fax machine. This story of survival takes a look at a modern horror.

The Kents by John Ostrander et al.—DC Comics, ISBN: 1–56389–513–7, $19.95. This historical western features the ancestors of Superman's foster father, and deals with Kansas from 1854 to 1874. This covers "Bleeding Kansas," the Civil War, and even Jesse James.

Kurt Busiek's Astro City—written by Kurt Busiek and Brent Anderson. DC Comics publishes these superhero books, set mainly in the metropolitan Astro City. They are often told from other points of view, such as that of the villain, or civilians. The collections are:

Life in the Big City, ISBN: 1–56389–551–X, $19.95 (SC).

Confession, ISBN: 1–56389–550–1, $19.95 (SC).

Family Ties, ISBN: 1–56389–552–8, $19.95 (SC).

Tarnished Angel, ISBN: 1–56389–653–2, $29.95 (SC).

Marvels, by Kurt Busiek and Alex Ross—Marvel Comics, ISBN: 0–785–10049–0, $19.95. The early days of the Marvel Universe as seen through the eyes, and lens, of photographer Phil Sheldon.

Maus: A Survivor's Tale—a Pulitzer Prize–winning tale by Art Speigelman. It tells of his father's experiences in the Holocaust. There are two volumes published by Random House.

Maus: A Survivor's Tale, Vol. 1: My Father Bleeds History, ISBN: 0–394–74723–2, $14.00 (SC).

Maus: A Survivor's Tale, Vol. 2: And Here My Troubles Began, ISBN: 0–679–72977–1, $14.00 (SC).

Pedro and Me: Friendship, Loss, & What I Learned by Judd Winick—Henry Holt, ISBN: 0–805–06403–6, $15.00. When Winick was on MTV's *The Real World,* his roommate was Pedro Zamora, an HIV-positive Cuban immigrant who later died of AIDS. Winick tells both of their stories in this award-winning book.

Sandman—Neil Gaiman's award-winning series fantasy about the God of Dreams from DC Comics. Some of the story lines in the 10-volume set feature him, while others feature mortals (and other beings) who may encounter him. This is a mature audience book, but it is a wonderful addition to any collection. The 10 volumes, some in hardcover, are:

> *The Sandman: Preludes and Nocturnes,* ISBN: 1–56389–011–9, $19.95 (SC).
>
> *The Sandman: The Doll's House,* ISBN: 0–930289–59–5, $19.95 (SC).
>
> *The Sandman: Dream County,* ISBN: 1–56389–226–X, $29.95 (HC); ISBN: 1–56389–016–X, $14.95 (SC); includes the script for one story.
>
> *The Sandman: Season of Mists,* ISBN: 1–56389–041–0, $19.95 (SC).
>
> *The Sandman: A Game of You,* ISBN: 1–56389–093–3, $29.95 (HC); ISBN: 1–56389–089–5, $19.95 (SC).
>
> *The Sandman: Fables and Reflections,* ISBN: 1–56389–106–9, $29.95 (HC); ISBN: 1–56389–105–0, $19.95 (SC).
>
> *The Sandman: Brief Lives,* ISBN: 1–56389–138–7, $19.95 (SC).
>
> *The Sandman: World's End,* ISBN: 1–56389–171–9, $19.95 (SC).
>
> *The Sandman: The Kindly Ones,* ISBN: 1–56389–205–7, $19.95 (SC).
>
> *The Sandman: The Wake,* ISBN: 1–56389–287–1, $29.95 (HC); ISBN: 1–56389–279–0, $19.95 (SC).
>
> There are also two spin-offs featuring the Sandman's sister, Death, as well as some other characters from the Sandman series.
>
> *Death: The High Cost of Living,* ISBN: 1–56389–133–6, $12.95 (SC).
>
> *Death: The Time of Your Life,* ISBN: 1–56389–333–9, $12.95 (SC).

Spider-Man—One of Marvel Comic's oldest characters, Spider-Man has a number of graphic novels and trade collections. Recent collections have included some excellent stories by authors Paul Jenkins and J. Michael Straczynski. Two other recent collections are:

> *Spider-Man: Tangled Web* by various authors and artists, ISBN: 0–7851–0803–3, $15.95. A collection from an anthology series, this book features both stand-alone and multipart stories.
>
> *Ultimate Spider-Man* by Brian Michael Bendis et al., ISBN: 0–785–11061–5, $29.99 (HC).

> *Ultimate Spider-Man, Vol. 1: Power and Responsibility*, ISBN: 0–785–10786–X, $14.95 (SC).
>
> *Ultimate Spider-Man, Vol. 2: Learning Curve*, ISBN: 0–785–10820–3, $14.95 (SC).

These provide a reimagining of Spider-Man, existing separately from the events of the other Spider-Man titles. They have been very popular among teens and younger ages.

Star Wars—There are many Trade Collections set in the Star Wars Universe, published mainly by Dark Horse Comics. Characters range from the major characters, to minor supporting characters, to new ones altogether. *Star Wars Tales* is an anthology series from Dark Horse, which features both serious and humorous stories. The comic has been collected in:

> *Star Wars Tales (Vol. 1)*, ISBN: 1–56971–619–6, $19.95 (SC).
>
> *Star Wars Tales (Vol. 2)*, ISBN: 1–56971–757–5, $19.95 (SC).

Static Shock: Trial by Fire by Dwayne McDuffie and Robert L. Washington—DC Comics, ISBN: 1–56389–746–6, $9.95. This book tells of the adventures of African-American teen hero Static. This reprints the first four issues of the comic series, which was a three-time winner of a Parent's Choice Award and the basis for a popular cartoon series.

Tale of One Bad Rat by Bryan Talbot—Dark Horse Comics, ISBN: 1–56971–077–5, $14.95. Many librarians have considered this collection to be a "must have" for their library collections. It tells the story of Helen Potter, who runs away from her sexually abusive father. A fan of Beatrix Potter, Helen retraces the author's steps in an attempt to get her own life together. Part of the book features Beatrix Potter–like artwork. Recommended for mature readers.

The Wizard's Tale by Kurt Busiek and David T. Wenzel—WildStorm/DC Comics, ISBN: 1–88727–934–2, $19.95. The story of Bafflerog Rumplewhisker, an evil wizard who somehow can't manage to be that evil, and his half-hearted quest to retrieve the legendary and powerful Book of Worse.

REFERENCE LIST

McCloud, Scott. *Reinventing Comics*. New York: HarperCollins, 2000.

3

TO READ, OR NOT TO READ: DEVELOPING AUDIOBOOK COLLECTIONS FOR TEEN LISTENERS

Francisca Goldsmith

INTRODUCING THE ISSUES

Spoken-word recordings allow teenagers to gain access to a wide variety of literature and performance styles. While audiobooks can be "read" by those with limited vision or who lack proficiency in decoding print, they are also of great benefit to busy teens who are multitaskers, to teens interested in enjoying theater arts, and to teens who simply enjoy oral language. In group situations—whether as fellow passengers on a car trip or members in a classroom—the playing of an audiobook provides an immediately shared experience with literature. Such experiences encourage discussion and bonding among audience members.

This chapter will review and provide an introduction to audiobooks in libraries, as well as these additional themes:

- Surveying teens' needs and interests
- How to evaluate audiobooks for teens
- Budgets issues
- Marketing and merchandising the audiobook collection
- The special needs of teen listeners

- Notable titles
- Audiobook distributors

Currently, audiobook producers produce materials for teens in several formats, including cassette, compact disc, on-line, and the emerging technology of MP3 disc. While many individual titles may be available in only one or two of these formats, most teens have some degree of access to all of these formats (the latter two in computer labs, if not at home), so consider all four for placement within your teen collection.

The term "audiobook" is most conservatively used to identify the unabridged recording of a previously printed monograph, in which the text of the recording and that of the print are identical. However, a more generous use of the term "audiobook" takes into its purview a wider variety of spoken word recordings that are based on some written text. These would include radio and stage plays, selected short stories or poems brought together from diverse print sources into one recorded collection, and narrative literature adapted or dramatized so that it becomes a performance piece rather than an orally delivered text.

Audiobook abridgement is a lively topic no matter which audience is intended for the recording. Purists hold that libraries should eschew abridged audiobooks from their collections just as they "should" shun abridged books. However, rare is the library collection that holds no abridged print material, and for good reason: sometimes the reader needs to know only the main story, not the full range of subplots and minor characters, or the whole is an overwhelming bulk of scholarly profundity that can be justly repackaged for general lay readers in a manner that leaves the basic tenets intact while editing away the arguments of interest only to fellow scholars. The same is true in the audiobook field: there is, in fact, little room in libraries for consumer-oriented abridgements of bestsellers; however, the gently abridged reading of a classic may, in fact, make it more likely, rather than less, to win a new generation of readers to a traditional text once it has been heard and enjoyed in a somewhat bowdlerized fashion that keeps the pace briskly modern.

Developmentally, teenagers seem to live through as many as three audiobook-friendly lifetimes:

- that of their late childhood, in which mostly parents select from among children's classics (traditional and newer) and for whom adult-sounding narrators are accepted, even when portraying a youthful viewpoint;

• mid-adolescence, when a few teachers and parents might make audiobook suggestions, but during which age the listening teen seems to have little patience for mismatches between the reader or readers' purported identities and his or her apparent voice qualities; and

• the maturity of late adolescence, in which audiobook tastes, and independence in making selections, merge with those of the adult audience.

In recent years, more audiobook publishers have demonstrated an awareness of the prevailing literary and auditory tastes of junior and high school aged listeners. Audiobook selections for adults remain both broad and deep, and selection for children ranges through both the developmental and interest areas of nonreaders, emerging readers, and children old enough to sustain orientation within a text a couple of hundred pages long; however, only recently have these same publishers realized that teenagers want and need recorded texts of their own.

In response to the recognition of teenagers as audiobook listeners, or potential listeners, producers are bringing into audiobook format:

• new young adult literature, and somewhat older young adult books (that are still available in print);

• experimental recordings using a full cast of readers, and texts read or performed by their own authors;

• traditional classroom texts, and works tied to contemporary events.

Many audiobooks aimed at teens are produced with value-added contents, including forewords or afterwords spoken by the text's author, author interviews, and even brief attempts at reader's advisory notes. Packaging notes generally include at least the publication information for the foundation work, the name and some credit lines about the performer(s), and the length of the full running. More useful, however, are the recording notes that include each piece's running time (cassette side, CD track), especially when it is keyed to chapter numbers or other index of the recording's relationship to its print version. While identifying the reader or readers is as much required as identifying the author, teenaged listeners seem to have less allegiance to particular narrators than do adults, so this information is simply for bibliographic control rather than as of pertinent interest to most intended audience members.

COST CONSIDERATIONS

Audiobooks, with the exception of the few available for free on-line, tend to be among the most expensive materials under consideration for teen library collections. Not only is the initial outlay per title likely to run as high as $50 to $80, but parts break or become lost and must be replaced. Cassette recordings suffer from a variety of environmental hazards, including sluggish playback equipment that unreels or breaks the tape, hot weather that warps the plastic housing, and magnetically operated library security equipment that erases the magnetically charged sound on the tape. Compact disc audiobooks still have multiple parts that may or may not be returned with the package, but the discs tend to live through some of the cassette's hardships more efficiently. The emerging MP3 technology compresses what can be recorded on a single disc so that there are even fewer parts to go missing; however, beyond up-to-date computers and the newest home audiovisual equipment, playback capability isn't broad-based enough for an MP3 collection to address general teen audiobook needs in any but the most affluent and technologically sophisticated communities.

In contrast with the high cost, audiobooks are among the material type included in a library's collection that is least likely to be familiar to the intended users, and for which it is most difficult of any media to find published opinions by that audience. While a variety of periodicals, as well as commercial and public Web sites, sport teen comments on print materials, movies, electronic games, and music, spoken-word recordings for teens are, for the most part in libraries, selected by library staff on the basis of professional reviews in a relatively limited number of resources, most of which are not read by teenagers or even parents and teachers. The combination of high per unit cost, need for sometimes expensive upkeep, and uncertainty about whether real teens will want this material often leads to poorly supported audiobook collections for teens: too few items for individuals to find what they might like; too brief a shelf life if the upkeep can't be maintained; too little impact on the audience's awareness to grow any meaningful appreciation or demand.

SURVEYING LOCAL TEEN NEEDS AND INTERESTS

Before undertaking the creation of a new media collection, you would do well to clarify how effectively it might address the concerns of its intended audience.

- Is there a community of listeners here? Are children and/or adults successfully utilizing an audiobook collection geared for them?

- How is time spent here by the intended audience? Are their lives overflowing with school and extracurricular activities that limit their use of library materials to curriculum support? Or are there apparently an abundance of "empty hours" created by under-employment and absent parents?

- Is much time spent by this age group commuting by private car? By public transit? By foot or bicycle? (Safety concerns should pro-hibit the use of personal listening equipment by those engaged in the latter two modes.)

- What kind of print literature is popular here with this group? What kind of movies? Is there an active theater or other perform-ing arts interest among the group?

- What reading levels are represented among the group, and which of these levels are dominant? What is the preferred language, both for speaking and for reading?

- Which books seem to be assigned perennially at the local second-ary schools? Which books seem to be perennially popular among this age group?

- If there is an established teen advisory council, have they been offered sample audiobooks to discuss? What did they think of their listening experiences?

- Do neighboring libraries, whether public or school, offer teen-agers an audiobook collection? What have their experiences been with local youth and this format?

- Are there any local businesses that rent audiobooks to teenagers? Do they have any relevant information to share about who is making the teens' listening selections at the business (teens them-selves, parents, others)?

Generally, a library collection of audiobooks for teens should mirror the genres available to users in print format. However, teen and community informants may be able to make a good argument for at least starting with a somewhat skewed collection:

- Would it be most useful to have classics that are required reading for all, available in this format so that even nonreaders would have access to the content of challenging novels, poetry, and plays?
- Would it be most inviting to have materials otherwise unavailable (e.g., famous speeches) as the beginning point of a whole new format collection?
- Would this be a welcome way to introduce new American teens to English language listening and reading?

EVALUATING AUDIOBOOKS FOR TEENS

Audiobooks intended for teen library users should fall within the general collection development policies of the library. Like print books for teens, they must be measurable against some collection criteria, especially those concerning the specific title's appropriateness to the intended audience, its successful exploitation of the medium, and its physical durability to withstand use multiple times.

As with traditional book reviews, audiobook reviews offer expert opinion about the effectiveness of the title under review:

- the veracity of its facts if it is nonfiction and of its sensibility if it is fiction;
- the quality of its technical production;
- the suitability of any foundation work to representation in this format;
- the suitability of the reader to his or her assigned text; and
- the identification of any difficulties which may place the reviewed material into a particular ranking with others of its sort.

Appropriateness to the Intended Audience

Audiobooks intended for teen listeners (either largely or among other user groups) are reviewed in several print journals, including *AudioFile*, *Booklist*, *KLIATT*, *Publisher's Weekly*, *School Library Journal*, and *Voice of Youth Advocates*.

- *AudioFile's* preeminent mission is to provide professional reviews of spoken-word recordings; the paper subscription can be augmented with a subscription to the on-line journal, which includes archived reviews. *AudioFile* offers "Young Adult" as a category for selectors, in both its reviews and lists of topical recommended listening.

- *KLIATT* supplies librarians and language arts teachers working with adolescents of all ages with about 50 spoken-word recording reviews per bimonthly issue; most of its reviewers are librarians and teachers actively working in the field of youth service and literature. Each *KLIATT* review designates the title as one of interest to one or more categories of audience, including junior high, high school, and adult.

- *Voice of Youth Advocates* (*VOYA*) has only begun to offer its readers regular reviews of spoken-word recordings. *VOYA* has a reputation, however, for providing stellar professional reviews to those in the young adult field. Each *VOYA* review is ranked twice: for quality and separately for likely popularity.

For subscription information to the mentioned reviewing sources, contact:

AudioFile, published by AudioFile Publications, Inc., 37 Silver Street, POB 109, Portland, ME 04112-0109, 1-207-774-7563

Booklist, published by the American Library Association (ALA), 50 East Huron Street, Chicago, IL 60611-2795, 1-800-545-2433

Kliatt Paperback Guide, 33 Bay State Road, Wellesley, MA 02481-3244, 1-617-237-7577

Publisher's Weekly and *School Library Journal*, P.O. Box 16178, North Hollywood, CA 91615-6178, 1-800-278-2991

Voice of Youth Advocates (*VOYA*), 4501 Forbes Boulevard, Suite 200, Lanham, MD 20706-4346, 1-888-486-9297

Other journals provide regular reviews of spoken-word recordings sited to young adult listeners, but in much smaller quantity (fewer than a dozen per issue).

There are on-line reviews of audiobooks available as well. Some offer samplings from the work itself, which, while compelling, should not be used as a substitute for a full critical review. At this time, the AcqWeb's Directory of Publishers and Vendors (http://acqweb.library.vanderbilt. edu/acqweb/pubr/audio.html) is the most comprehensive on-line portal to audiobook resources, including smaller vendors and samples.

Reading reviews, however, is only a small part of discerning what is suitable for the audience for whom one is selecting. To create and maintain a solid spoken-word collection for teens, one must seek older materials that perhaps went unreviewed, as there are more review sources for audiobook selectors now than ever before, and one must also trace recordings that may not get national attention but that demand local consideration (as of a local professional acting troupe).

In order to understand the full implications of the terminology used by reviewers (e.g., "voicing," "color," "full cast"), listen to some audiobooks. It simply isn't wise to select in a format that you have never consumed as an end user. Learning to listen can be a bit tricky, especially for visually inclined learners/readers. Give each audiobook you try about half an hour before deciding that it is the production that isn't working, rather than the fact that your listening acuity hasn't warmed yet. Try, too, to listen to a variety of genres (poetry and drama, as well as fiction of varying lengths) produced by a variety of companies and read in a variety of styles.

Now you are ready to connect what you learned from your initial survey with your knowledge of what is available to be collected for your local teens. Revert to the information you have already gathered about your audiobook audience's tastes, needs, and abiltities, and use it to inform the criteria you design to assure that your collection is appropriate to your mission.

BUDGETING ISSUES

As has been noted, audiobooks are both expensive and prone to need replacement because of unintended damages incurred with typical library use. The budget for a teen audiobook collection must include an amount set aside with which to respond to those damages with replacement parts or with all-out replacement of a strongly circulating item. In a year, it is likely that a collection of 300 spoken-word recordings on cassette will require the total replacement of at least a dozen titles too mangled to be mended with replacement parts. Another 25 or so titles will require replacement parts. Some production companies provide these at a minimal cost ($3 to $5 per tape) when the replacement is required in the same year as purchase, while some companies provide it free.

Collections composed of mixed cassette/compact disc selections may suffer no fewer losses. This is because the perceptibly more "cutting-edge" CD format is likely to attract more active users and because compact discs become broken and lost and require replacement, too. Replacement compact discs may run as high as $7 each, the price of a new paperback. MP3 selections have fewer parts to become compromised, but it would be difficult to build a balanced collection for teens at this time using only MP3 selections. On-line audiobook recordings have no breakage or loss problems, but, even more dramatically than with MP3s, the overall title selection and heavy demand on technology make this format impractical as the single one of which to build teen collections.

Many audiobook publishers provide library purchasers with packaging that is both shelf-ready and hardy enough to survive many circulations. However, other production companies with goods that may appeal to the teen collection development specialist make no special arrangements for the library market; these purchases will have to be placed in separately ordered containers, which cost little (less than $5 a unit), but require the staff labor of refitting the container's holdings as well as the original container labeling. When new parts are ordered to replace those lost or damaged within an audiobook, there are concomitant processing costs as well. None of these add-ons should be neglected when the collection developer composes the budget necessary to acquire and maintain a collection.

MARKETING AND MERCHANDISING THE COLLECTION

The type of marketing necessary to move your audiobook collection from the shelf into its intended users' playback equipment varies with how much interest local youth have in both books and sound equipment. In some library situations, shelving audiobooks within the book collection—side by side with the same work, or similar works, in print format—proves ideal. Potential listeners see the option as they scan more familiar ones, and can choose between formats after considering both the degree of difficulty presented by the print text and the length of time required to hear it out.

Elsewhere, spoken-word recordings are so coveted by commuters and others relegated to social inactivitiy for extended periods that it is sensible to place titles together in a separate format area. Placing audiobooks that you hope will reach teen listeners among a collection set up to serve the needs of adult commuters will grant you high circulation, but probably not with teens.

When it comes to library displays, do not forget your audiobook collection. Either create separate audiobook displays, or include audiobook titles as part of the standard library book displays. One can do this by including the audiobook version of the written texts or by utilizing the audiobooks to complement the display. This cross-merchandising will have a positive effect on the circulation of audiobooks, as well as increasing awareness of the collection.

Cataloging should always reflect as much as is known about the recording:

- title
- author
- production company
- playback time
- format
- number of its parts
- the reader(s) involved
- the degree of faithfulness it maintains to a print text

While most audiobook users, including teens, do most if not all of their audiobook selection by shelf-browsing, public service staff needs access to catalog information in order to perform adequate reader's (or listener's, in this case) advisory work.

Cataloging, too, should reflect the subject(s) of the recording (as they would be reflected for print materials), and should use nomenclature that the public is likely to understand. The Library of Congress subject heading for audiobooks, for instance, is "audiobooks"; designating such items as "talking book," "sound cassette," or "book on tape" communicates to some, but certainly not the majority of teenaged listeners, especially those who are looking for material in a format other than cassette.

Lists of suggested topical reading for teens can include a standard ratio of titles held in the collection in audiobook format. This extends the list's utility among potential users and alerts print-bound readers to the availability of an alternative format by which to consume their favorite types of reading.

Discussions of how well the audiobooks are appreciated, or not, can be elicited through yet another marketing means, the book discussion group. Especially where audiobooks may be a new alternative to teen readers, it can help individuals to discern their own tastes if they participate in discussions of what works and what doesn't among the library's offerings. Ask your teen advisory group to sample your teen audiobook collection and come to the next meeting prepared to talk about both the qualities of the recording and the attractiveness of the particular selections recorded.

Be sure, too, to let other community agencies and adults who work with teens know about the collection. Classroom teachers are often (but not always) enthusiastic supporters of these materials, as audiobooks are perceived by many (but certainly not all) as a means of leveling the field of access to texts that are intrinsic to secondary school study. In addition to providing reluctant and underdeveloped (or non-English) print readers with access to the text, spoken-word recordings of such typically studied authors as William Shakespeare and Mark Twain improve comprehension for even accelerated students: unfamiliar turns of phrase are presented with correct rhythms and regional accents that can make slow sight-reading literally come to life.

TEEN LISTENERS HAVE SPECIAL LISTENING NEEDS

Selecting audiobooks for local teen listeners requires you to know about local tastes and interests. Listed below are some special needs that teenagers have as a separate demographic class.

Packaging

Publisher-produced packaging should be both discreet and sturdy, providing as much information as possible about playing time and correlation between cassette sides or compact disc tracks and any foundation text. If the recording includes an author interview or other such added-value material, that should be noted on the packaging as well; the choice between the print version and the recorded one may hinge on this added-value content, especially when the recording is for school use. If the library repackages audiobooks in processing for circulation, the publisher-supplied information should be copied to the new package.

Pacing and Length

Teenagers are relatively unaccustomed to sustaining audience attention to works of great length. Commuting adults have taught themselves to attend to books that require more than a dozen cassettes to hear, but in general, teenagers seem less willing to hear out a book across more than six or eight hours. Teenagers who are new audiobook listeners, especially, seem to find that fast-paced texts that run no more than four hours meet their comfort level best.

Narration

Teenagers are less likely than adults to suffer through a recording in which the narrator seems to be mismatched in age or ethnicity with the text. Children are typically uncritical of narrators who sound fully adult, even when portraying youthful speakers, but teenagers view such mismatching as sufficient reason to reject the recording out of hand.

Reluctant Readers Turned Listeners

Teenagers who are reluctant or underdeveloped readers can be inspired to listen to books that their reading peers find compelling. This means that what is a good selection for the teen audiobook collection may be adult fantasy or science fiction or, more difficult to find in audiobook format, newly emerging niche market and paperback authors. (Audiobooks are also wonderful tools for teens who are learning to speak and read English. The pairing of a book's print and audio version is an especially effective approach.)

Independence

The experience of sharing a book as it is being read (whether in recorded format or by reading printed text aloud) can be powerful in its intimacy, and teens planning to go on a family trip, or in a class situation can appreciate the group experience. But there are many audiobooks appropriate for teenagers that aren't good fits for family or even group listening. Teenagers, whenever and however possible, should have equipment available that allows them to listen independently. Acquaint yourself with audiobooks in both categories, and be prepared to recommend appropriately. Reviews sometimes identify material as appropriate for family listening, a comment that should be passed along to potential audiobook borrowers during the reader's advisory exchange. These titles do offer listeners something to discuss across generations, but should not be the only material available to listeners who are working to achieve intellectual independence, as part of the adolescent maturing process.

PERIPHERAL ISSUES

Building and maintaining a collection of spoken-word recordings for young adults implies that the intended audience can access the collection and that the collection justly serves them.

Intellectual Freedom

If community standards are such that printed materials are regularly challenged because of language, realize that the charge is likely to be even more readily made when the offending words are recorded. Especially where teenagers cannot enjoy listening privacy, recordings may be challenged because of their use of profanity, ethnic slurs, or even regional accents. Heard aloud, any of these possibly objectionable intonements can indeed pack a more powerful punch than it may have in print. If your library's video policy is constructed to reduce objections about youth exposure to adult language, correlate your spoken-word recording policy with that (and then work with your community to educate everyone about intellectual freedom's tenets!).

Physical Access

Teenagers in the United States typically have access to playback sound equipment that is cutting edge, in contrast with older and younger family members. If local teenagers all own personal compact disc players with no cassette option, then building a spoken-word recording collection that is overwhelmingly in cassette format just isn't well-conceived. On the other hand, if there are no listening stations in your library at which youth can hear MP3 format recordings, it's still a bit soon to assume that the majority of your users will be able to access the format when they take it home. Some, in fact, do have that ability now, however, so be sure to include the option if it fits into your budget and long-term plans to expand the collection as technology changes. Check to see which formats are best suited to your teen patrons, and design your collection accordingly.

Allow Responsible Borrowing

Because of the cost and likelihood of replacing parts in any spoken-word recording collection, make it clear to its users that special care is required. Include information in publicly available formats about replacement part billing for lost and damaged cassettes and compact discs. Be sure that each separate part of a multipart recording is marked with the item-level bar code or other means of tracking the correct replacement of fugitive parts. Post clear signage on return bins and automatic checkout equipment if they are unsuited to use with recorded materials. When discussing the collection with individual library users or with groups when you are performing outreach, include mention of the fact that audiobooks require especially attentive care on the part of any borrower who wants to remain unencumbered by charges for damage or loss.

Practice what you are preaching by taking care of the materials when they are in the library's hold. Follow up on user complaints that cassettes are muffled and replace them if your equipment, which is, of course, in good shape, shows that the quality of the part has indeed degraded. Clean compact discs as needed, and replace disc sleeves and exterior packaging when they become damaged and compromise the borrower's ability to keep parts secure and/or read packaging information.

Keep Up With the Future

Format decisions made today need to be revisited on a regular basis. Not only does technology change the options available to audiobook listeners, but production companies change editorial and library business directions. Listen to visiting audiobook salespeople as they explain these changes, and ask questions about how you can work with various companies to be most cost-effective, while maintaining choice quality, in your local situation. Also, of course, communities and the needs of potential library users change; an audiobook collection that succeeded when the neighborhood comprised monolingual English speakers is going to need revamping as the area diversifies, for instance.

SPECIAL SPOKEN-WORD COLLECTIONS FOR TEENS

Small Starter Collecting

Audiobooks recorded on cassette or compact disc that are appropriate to young adult audiences generally cost between $25 and $90 per title. In order to purchase sufficient numbers of titles to represent both breadth of options and depth in areas heavily favored by local youth, consider that it could cost at least $15,000, with one year's replacement and some extra packaging purchases included. This is not an inexpensive initial outlay for a new audiobook collection, although the collection would contain young adult and some adult fiction, such nonfiction as biographies and collected essays, and standard high school curriculum classics.

If your library's financial situation is such that you would prefer to experiment with a less expensive collection, consider designing a tightly focused one that will enjoy wide usage by the target group. For instance, many archival tapes of famous poets reading their own works are available in single compact disc or cassette format at modest prices. Shakespeare's plays, which continue to be assigned to 21st century American high school students, are also available—in nicely produced full cast recordings—at costs equivalent to those of new hardcover young adult books. Collections of famous speeches, other popular stage plays, and collections of short stories generally can be found in audiobook format at relatively inexpensive per title prices. Once you have begun to "grow" a teen audience for spoken-word recordings, you may have an easier time justifying the heady cost of buying a broader collection.

However, if you choose to focus narrowly, be sure that your marketing strategies match the focal area. You should remember, too, to obtain enough copies of materials that teens who come to the collection after its opening day still have a chance to succeed in finding something available before the end of the initial loan period.

Exploring Offerings from Abroad

Although audiobooks seem to be less universal in both availability and popular understanding than print materials like newspapers and other recorded materials like music, the United States is not the only place to shop for satisfying teen listening. At this time, one major American production company in the library market (Recorded Books) offers adult Spanish-language audiobooks. Some of these materials, which are recorded in Latin American Spanish, are suitable for teen listeners.

On the other side of the Pacific Rim, Australia participates in the audiobook market with considerable attention to young adult listeners. Like American print book publishers—and among American audiobook publishers, Random House's Listening Library imprint—producers of Australian audiobooks market specifically to teens of various ages, just as they do to younger children and to mature adults. Most of these Australian recordings (from Bolinda Audio and also from the Louis Braille Society of Australia) are performed by readers with very light and clearly understood accents. Many themes popular in Australian young adult fiction resonate with American teens: developing independence, family identity, insider/outsider struggles, school stories, and social and health issues (including teen pregnancy).

Keeping a Lookout for the Very Local

Many places in the United States support local acting troupes, storytelling societies, and other groups who produce recordings of their performances. Building a collection of these offers teens access to events for which they may not be able to afford admission. It also can inspire nascent actors and storytellers to become involved in honing their craft.

Events that involve local teens, especially those in which they perform in the library (poetry readings, for instance), can be recorded, cataloged, and made available to borrowers. This is a relatively simple and inexpensive way of promoting youth activity and your budding audiobook collection simultaneously.

LISTS OF NOTABLE AUDIOBOOKS FOR TEEN LISTENERS

Notable lists composed by YALSA (first under the aegis of the Media Selection and Usage Committee and now through the renamed Audio Books and Alternative Media Exploration Committee) can be viewed at http://www.ala.org/yalsa/booklists, and click on the Selected Audiobooks link. Each year, the new list is published at ALA Midwinter. Spoken-word recordings produced during the past two years are eligible for this list.

The committee selects titles based on their appeal to a teen audience and on the quality of their recording, and because they enhance the audience's appreciation of any written work on which they may be based. The list addresses the interests and needs of young adults ranging in age from 12 to 18; individual titles may appeal to parts of that range rather than to its whole. The following lists are reprinted with permission of the Young Adult Library Services Association, a division of the American Library Association.

The 1999 List

Blood and Chocolate, by Annette Curtis Klause, read by Alyssa Bresnahan, Recorded Books, 1998.

Brave New World, by Aldous Huxley, read by Michael York, Audio Partners, 1998.

Down River, by Will Hobbs, read by Christina Moore, Recorded Books, 1997.

Freak the Mighty, by Rodman Philbrick, read by Elden Henson, Listening Library, 1998.

Into Thin Air, by Jon Krakauer, read by the author, Bantam Doubleday Dell, 1988.

Lives of the Presidents, by Kathleen Krull, read by John C. Brown, Audio Bookshelf, 1998.

Out of the Dust, by Karen Hesse, read by Martha Mashburn, Listening Library, 1998.

Parrot in the Oven: Mi Vida, by Victor Martinez, read by the author, HarperAudio, 1998.

Walk Two Moons, by Sharon Creech, read by Kate Harper, Listening Library, 1997.

Wasted, by Marya Hornbacher, read by the author, Bantam Doubleday Dell, 1998.

Weeping Willow, by Ruth White, read by Angela Jayne Rogers, Recorded Books, 1997.

Whistling Toilets, The, by Randy Powell, read by Johnny Heller, Recorded Books, 1997.

The 2000 List

Edgar Allen Poe's Stories and Tales I, Monterey SoundWorks, adapted by Michael Sollazzo, 1998.

The Golden Compass, by Phillip Pullman, read by a full cast, Listening Library, 1999.

Habibi, by Naomi Shihab Nye, read by Christina Moore, Recorded Books, 1999.

Harry Potter and the Chamber of Secrets, by J.K. Rowling, read by Jim Dale, Listening Library, 1999.

Harry Potter and the Sorcerer's Stone, by J.K. Rowling, read by Jim Dale, Listening Library, 1999.

Holes, by Louis Sachar, read by Kerry Beyer, Listening Library, 1999.

I Am Mordred: A Tale from Camelot, by Nancy Springer, read by Stephen Crossley, Recorded Books, 1999.

In My Hands: Memories of a Holocaust Rescuer, by Irene Gut Opdyke with Jennifer Armstrong, read by Hope Davis, Bantam Doubleday Audio, 1999.

Jesse, by Gary Soto, read by Robert Ramirez, Recorded Books, 1999.

Legends: Stories by the Masters of Fantasy, Vol. 2, edited by Robert Silverberg, HarperAudio, 1998.

Lena, by Jacqueline Woodson, read by Kate Forbes, Recorded Books, 1999.

Life in the Fat Lane, by Cherie Bennett, read by Christina Moore, Recorded Books, 1998.

A Long Way from Chicago, by Richard Peck, read by Ron McLarty, Listening Library, 1999.

My Louisiana Sky, by Kimberly Willis, read by Judith Ivey, Listening Library, 1998.

Pretty Fire, written and performed by Charlayne Woodard, L.A. Theatre Works, 1999.

Red Scarf Girl: A Memoir of the Cultural Revolution, by Ji Li Jiang, read by Christina Moore, Recorded Books, 1999.

Sang Spell, by Phyllis Reynolds Naylor, read by Ron Rifkin, Listening Library, 1999.

Six Adventures of Tintin Vol. 1, by Herge, read by a full cast, Listening Library, 1999.

Soldier's Heart, by Gary Paulsen, read by George Wendt, Bantam Doubleday Dell Audio, 1998.

Switchers, by Kate Thomas, read by Niamh Cusack, Listening Library, 1999.

There's a Girl in My Hammerlock, by Jerry Spinelli, read by Julie Dretzin, Recorded Books, 1999.

The Upstairs Room, by Johanna Reiss, read by Christina Moore, Recorded Books, 1999.

Whispers from the Dead, by Joan Lowery Nixon, read by Julie Dretzin, Recorded Books, 1999.

Z for Zachariah, by Robert O'Brien, read by Christina Moore, Recorded Books, 1999.

The 2001 List

Buried Onions, by Gary Soto, read by Robert Ramirez, Recorded Books, 2001.

Edith's Story: Courage, Love and Survival During World War II, by Edith Velmans, read by Miriam Margoyles, Audio Partners, 2000.

Fever 1793, by Laurie Halse Anderson, read by Emmy Bergl, Listening Library, 2000.

The Folk Keeper, by Franny Billingsley, read by Marian Thomas Griffin, Listening Library, 2000.

Frenchtown Summer, by Robert Cormier, read by Rene Auberjonois, Listening Library, 2000.

Gathering Blue, by Lois Lowry, read by Katherine Borowitz, Listening Library, 2000.

Harry Potter and the Goblet of Fire, by J.K. Rowling, read by Jim Dale, Listening Library, 2000.

Harry Potter and the Prisoner of Azkaban, by J.K. Rowling, read by Jim Dale, Listening Library, 2000.

Just Tricking!, by Andy Griffiths, read by Stig Wemyss, Bolinda Audio, 1999.

Lockie Leonard: Human Torpedo, by Tim Winton, read by Stig Wemyss, Bolinda Audio, 1998 (released in United States, 2000).

Looking for Alibrandi, by Melina Marchetta, read by Marcella Russo, Bolinda Audio, 1999.

Monster, by Walter Dean Myers, read by full cast, Listening Library, 2000.

Shakespeare: His Life and Work, by Richard Hampton and David Weston, read by the authors with performances from 33 plays by Judi Dench and Timothy West, Audio Partners, 2000.

Sherlock's Secret Life, by Ed Lange, narrated by Karl Malden and performed by the New York State Theatre Institute, New York State Theatre Institute, 1999.

Sitting Bull and His World, by Albert Marvin, read by Ed Sala, Recorded Books, 2001 (released in United States, 2000).

Slake's Limbo, by Felice Holman, read by Neil Patrick Harris, Listening Library, 2000.

Speak, by Laurie Halse Anderson, read by Mandy Siegfried, Listening Library, 2000.

The Subtle Knife, by Philip Pullman, narrated by Philip Pullman with a full cast, Listening Library, 2000.

To Kill a Mockingbird, by Harper Lee, read by Roses Prichard, Audio Partners, 2000.

Tomorrow, When the War Began, by John Marsden, read by Suzi Dougherty, Bolinda Audio, 1999.

Walker's Crossing, by Phyllis Reynolds Naylor, read by Tom Wopat, Listening Library, 2000.

Wild: Stories of Survival from the World's Most Dangerous Places, by various authors, edited by Clint Willis, read by Albert Coia, Richard Rohan, and Nick Sampson, Listen & Live Audio, 2000.

Williwaw!, by Tom Bodett, read by the author, Listening Library, 2000.

The 2002 List

Bad Boy: A Memoir, by Walter Dean Myers, read by Joe Morton, HarperAudio, 2001.

Borrowed Light, by Anna Fienberg, read by Rebecca Macauley, Bolinda Audio, 2000.

Cut, by Patricia McCormick, read by Clea Lewis, Listening Library, 2001.

Esperanza Rising, by Pam Munoz Ryan, read by Trini Alvarado, Listening Library, 2001.

Give a Boy a Gun, by Todd Strasser, read by various narrators, Recorded Books, 2001.

The Grey King, by Susan Cooper, read by Richard Mitchley, Listening Library, 2001.

Homeless Bird, by Gloria Whelan, read by Sarita Choudhury, Listening Library, 2001.

Killing Aurora, by Helen Barnes, read by Suzi Dougherty, Bolinda Audio, 2000.

The Land, by Mildred D. Taylor, read by Ruben Santiago-Hudson, Listening Library, 2001.

The Last Book in the Universe, by Rodman Philbrick, read by Jeremy Davies, Listening Library, 2001.

The Member of the Wedding, by Carson McCullers, performed by a full cast, L.A. Theatre Works, 2001.

Miracle's Boys, by Jacqueline Woodson, read by Dule Hill, Listening Library, 2001.

Out of the Shadows, by Sue Hines, read by Caroline Lee, Bolinda Audio, 2001.

A Series of Unfortunate Events: The Bad Beginning, by Lemony Snicket, read by Tim Curry, Listening Library, 2001.

A Series of Unfortunate Events: The Reptile Room, by Lemony Snicket, read by Tim Curry, Listening Library, 2001.

Shipwreck at the Bottom of the World, by Jennifer Armstrong, read by Taylor Mali, Audio Bookshelf, 2000.

The Sisterhood of the Traveling Pants, by Ann Brashares, read by Angela Goethals, Listening Library, 2001.

Stargirl, by Jerry Spinelli, read by John Ritter, Listening Library, 2001.

Strange Objects, by Gary Crew, read by Stig Wemyss, Bolinda Audio, 2000.

Stuck in Neutral, by Terry Trueman, read by Johnny Heller, Recorded Books, 2001.

Tangerine, by Edward Bloor, read by Ramon de Ocampo, Recorded Books, 2001.

Touching Spirit Bear, by Ben Mikaelsen, read by Lee Tergesen, Listening Library, 2001.

Walden, by Henry David Thoreau, read by William Hope, NAXOS Audiobooks, 2001.

When Kambia Elaine Flew in from Neptune, by Lori Aurelia Williams, read by Heather Alicia Simms, Listening Library, 2001.

Witch Child, by Celia Rees, read by Jennifer Ehle with Carole Shelley, Listening Library, 2001.

The 2003 List

All-American Girl, by Meg Cabot, read by Ariadne Meyers, Listening Library, 2002.

The Beetle and Me: A Love Story, by Karen Romano Young, read by Julie Dretzin, Recorded Books, 2001.

Breathing Underwater, by Alex Flinn, read by Jon Cryer, Listening Library, 2002.

Catalyst, by Laurie Halse Anderson, read by Samantha Mathis, Listening Library, 2002.

Devil's Island, by David Harris, read by Peter Hardy, Bolinda Audio, 2001.

Firehouse, by David Halberstam, read by Mel Foster, Brilliance-Audio, 2001.

Forged by Fire, by Sharon M. Draper, read by Thomas Penny, Recorded Books, 2002.

A Girl of the Limberlost, by Gene Stratton-Porter, read by Christina Moore, Recorded Books, 2001.

Hoot, by Carl Hiaasen, read by Chad Lowe, Listening Library, 2002.

Lirael, by Garth Nix, read by Tim Curry, Listening Library, 2002.

Make Lemonade, by Virginia Euwer Wolff, read by Heather Alicia Simms, Listening Library, 2002.

Martin Luther King, Jr., by Marshall Frady, read by the author, Books on Tape, 2002.

The Rag and Bone Shop, by Robert Cormier, read by Scott Shina, Recorded Books, 2002.

Sabriel, by Garth Nix, read by Tim Curry, Listening Library, 2002.

The Secret Armies: Spies, Counterspies, and Saboteurs in World War II, by Albert Marrin, read by Johnny Heller, Recorded Books, 2001.

The Seeing Stone, by Kevin Crossley-Holland, read by Michael Maloney, Listening Library, 2001.

Seek, by Paul Fleischman, dramatized by Ben Fred, David Minnick, Kari Wishingrad, Vonya Morris, Richard Goodman, Randi Merzon, Anne Galjour, and Clark Taylor, Listening Library, 2002.

A Separate Peace, by John Knowles, read by Scott Snively, Audio Bookshelf, 2002.

A Single Shard, by Linda Sue Park, read by Graeme Malcolm, Listening Library, 2002.

Son of the Mob, by Gordon Korman, read by Max Casella, Listening Library, 2002.

Spite Fences, by Trudy Krisher, read by Kate Forbes, Recorded Books, 2001.

A Step from Heaven, by An Na, read by Jina Oh, Listening Library, 2002.

Time Stops for No Mouse: A Hermux Tantamoq Adventure, by Michael Hoeye, read by Campbell Scott, Listening Library, 2002.

True Believer, by Virginia Euwer Wolff, read by Heather Alicia Simms, Listening Library, 2002.

Troy, by Adèle Geras, read by Miriam Margolyes, Listening Library, 2002.

Whale Talk, by Chris Crutcher, read by Brian Corrigan, Listening Library, 2002.

The Witch in the Lake, by Anna Fienberg, read by Melissa Eccleston, Louis Braille Audio, 2001.

Wolf on the Fold, by Judith Clarke, read by Dino Marnika, Bolinda Audio, 2001.

Zazoo, by Richard Mosher, read by Joanna Wyatt, Listening Library, 2002.

Scanning library Web-based catalogs is another way to create your own shopping or wish lists. This can be tricky because libraries use a variety of material type tagging to label their audiobook collections. Easiest to check are those library catalogs where the term "audiobook" is always listed as one of the subject headings, or where a catalog search can be limited to material type and "audiobook" is an option.

AUDIOBOOK COMPANIES FOR YOUNG ADULT COLLECTORS

Book publishers occasionally produce audiobook versions simultaneously with new print publications by noted young adult authors. Consumer-oriented audiobook producers also address the interests of young adult library collection developers on an occasional basis. However, the following production companies offer broad and deep audiobook selections of interest to teens on an ongoing basis.

- Audio Bookshelf (http://www.audiobookshelf.com) produces and distributes unabridged audiobooks for all ages. Their high school oriented selections include American classics, contemporary young adult fiction, poetry, and nonfiction (mostly biography).

- Bolinda Audio (http://www.bolinda.com) is an Australian production company whose cassettes and tapes are distributed in the United States by Landmark Audiobooks (http://www.landmark

audio.com). Bolinda's stable of readers used in their young adult recording sound teenaged themselves (in tone). The books on which the recordings are based are Australian contemporary fiction, ranging from problem novels to adventure to humor. Bolinda also produces audiobooks for children and for adults.

- L.A. Theatre Works (http://www.latw.org) records its productions of a wide variety of stage plays. Contemporary playwrights, as well as those who have been in the secondary school canon for a century or more, are represented by professional stage actors who have name recognition among teenaged drama arts students, teachers, and librarians.

- Listen & Live Audio (http://www.listenandlive.com) produces mostly adult materials, but many are of interest to older teens. These include thematic compilations taken from both fiction and nonfiction works about such adventures as working with fire, mountain climbing, and taking to the high seas.

- Listening Library (http://www.randomhouse.com/audio/listeninglibrary) is the youth imprint partnered with adult Books On Tape (http://www.booksontape.com). Listening Library's offerings include a wide range of literary young adult fiction, including series fantasy and books that have won recent ALA-sponsored awards. Listening Library's large stable of multiethnic readers offers listeners a diversity of vocal styles. Packaging offers extensive indexing between the recording and the print text on which it is based. Although Audio Bookshelf (above) and Recorded Books (below) also have made a few full-cast recordings for teen listeners, and Bruce Coville's new spoken word recording company, Full Cast Audio (http://www.fullcastaudio.com), limits its work to just this type for children, Listening Library's occasional full-cast young adult productions stand out as consistently inspired and inspiring.

- NAXOS Audiobooks (http://www.naxosaudiobooks.com) offers teen listeners accessible productions of classics, including nonfiction as well as short story collections. While some of these are gently abridged, they bring new life to texts too often relegated to narrow-margined paperbacks with print too fine to invite careful reading except by the most studious high schooler.

- Recorded Books (http://www.recordedbooks.com) is the giant in the spoken-word recording field in most library circles. The company offers both broad and deep selections appropriate to young adult listeners, but label all their titles as either for children or for adults, so young adult selectors must consider both realms and glean from them. Because the company relies on actors only in New York City, productions narrated in youthful-sounding—or ethnic-flavored—voices tend to use the same readers frequently.

4

TUNES AND TEENS: A NO-NONSENSE GUIDE

Melanie Rapp-Weiss

How can the passion of music be the thorn of torment to librarians? Music is always changing, opinions are everlasting, and the controversy is always, always brewing! The fear of the unknown lingers like a poorly tuned guitar:

- Why should there be music in the teen collection?
- How will I ever keep up?
- Will parents complain because of the parental advisory sticker?
- What does the parental advisory sticker mean?
- How can I claim to understand the music when the lyrics cause me to have a parental flinch?
- How do I keep CDs from being stolen?
- How do I make my library collection appealing to teens?
- Programs on teen music? Help!

A "hip" and current music collection is the ultimate key to attracting teens to the library. Teens who would not dream of touching a book will rush to the library to check out the latest CD. Music is a major part of a teen's life. It offers vitality, a sense of belonging, and a connection to everyday life. Music is the language of a teenager. It expresses personality, spirit, and style. Music can also be the defining factor to prove or gain popularity or to establish peer status. Many teens associate themselves with peers according to the music they listen to: country, metal, hip-hop, thrash, Goth, techno, rap, boy and girl bands, alternative, the list goes on . . .

Digital Music Revolution

Digital Music is an exciting, up-and-coming way of listening to music downloaded from the Internet. Once you have downloaded music from a computer onto a CD-R (recordable) or CD-RW (re-writable) CD, you can play these discs on various devices. These devices include MP3 players, your own computer, compact disc players, handheld jukeboxes, and DVD players, to name just a few. Music can also be downloaded onto music playback modules, totally surpassing the use of a disc. Digital music is an important trend in the music industry.

Many music companies are having financial difficulties because customers aren't buying music CDs as they were originally marketed. What does this mean to a teen librarian and why is it important? This knowledge will help you communicate with teens. This is really cool stuff, and is addictive once you get the fever! So, ask teens how they get their music. You may be surprised that some know a lot about the new trends and some may not care.

This will also impact how you buy music for your collection. When a teen can download music at a few keystrokes, will they visit the library to check out a CD? Will they be patient enough to wait a few weeks while reserves clear or the CD is processed? You will have to market your music collection keeping these things in mind. Many experts feel that CDs are perhaps on their way out. Their cost is relatively high and they can be limited in format. How do you keep up with all these changes? Visit your local music stores and audio stores, read the Sunday paper ads, cruise the Internet, and so forth. This is an exciting time, and even more so if you have a grasp of where music technology is going!

In this chapter, I will offer ideas, insights, and helpful hints for building and maintaining a teen music collection. I also will provide you with information on music trends and censorship issues, as well as questions to ask yourself when building or developing a music collection for teens.

Because of this, your comfort level may be challenged and stretched within the following pages. I do this so you won't let a mediocre teen music collection be a regret—make a successful collection a reality!

WHY SHOULD YOU INCLUDE MUSIC IN YOUR TEEN COLLECTION?

This point is often pondered between teens, teen librarians, and library administration. Music brings teens into the library and keeps them coming back. Many teens like to listen to music before they buy it or spend the time downloading the music from the Internet. Music in the library also offers teens opportunities to listen to music that they otherwise wouldn't experience. Music is a form of entertainment, enrichment, and library interest. Just as the library offers nursery rhymes for children and business and stock reports for adults, there should be music for teens.

Next time you go to a shopping mall, notice the consumer focus on teens. Music stores, clothing stores, perfume kiosks, accessory shops, and the like are all designed and decorated to appeal to teens. If, as libraries, we want to serve our teen customers, we must provide what they want and satisfy their interests. We have *a lot* of competition.

Besides the shopping mall, let's look at a few of these competitors. Television is teen-oriented. Many teen-oriented shows highlight the music played throughout the program during the show-ending credits. Music groups and artists gain popularity with this type of exposure. Many times teens go to the library in search of a new group featured on their favorite television show. Commercials are marketing catchy popular songs to promote their products. Car, snack, and cereal commercials and even televised political campaigns have a popular song playing in the background. Musicians and groups are constantly highlighted in popular culture magazines, which also feature perfume advertisements, shoes, and biographies of their life experiences. Musicians are looked upon as role models and can spark teens into reading! Artists have certainly crossed over into cameo appearances and large movie roles. Actors have turned into musicians! Both actors and musicians are authors! Entertainment is entertainment; there are no boundaries.

As I was cruising through the Internet, I found a Web site with a question that took teen music to a whole new level. The question was, "What if our government was run like MTV?" One of the answers was:

"No more elections, you choose by calling in." Imagine the possibilities for the future! Music leads society to a place of fulfillment and defines the attitudes of generations that eventually lead to everyday practice.

The evolution of popularity changes, not to mention that music format has been revolutionary throughout the years. The 45 record to the 33 record to eight-tracks to cassette tapes to CDs to previews and downloads of music off the Internet to MP3 disks to . . . what's next? Music and music format define history. It all changes with the times! As libraries, we must welcome the changes with the times in order to serve our library customers who support the library's existence.

COLLECTION DEVELOPMENT POLICY

A collection development manual for your library should specifically include music selection. This is the first and most vital step to providing a successful teen music collection. Collection development policies build a strong library environment because they encourage staff and patrons to be on the same page. If you are creating a music selection policy, investigate different policies from different library systems, especially if you are writing one from scratch. Keep your library board informed of your music selections in regard to your selection policy. The more communication, the better! Support and availability of information will keep a clear focus of purchasing, maintaining, and promoting teen music at your library.

Your collection development policy section on music should reflect the following:

- How local interests will be respected and focused upon when choosing music.
- What music will be in the library for both cultural and recreational use.
- A provision stating the library will select and own diverse music.
- Popular materials and community requested items will be purchased for the library.
- All points of view will be expressed through the collection.

Be sure to keep your collection development policy available for easy referral! And review your policy every two years, both as a reminder and to evaluate content.

MUSIC GENRES—WHAT ARE THEY?

There are many types of genres in the music world. They are ever-changing and often challenged. For example, some music groups cross over from country to pop, and so on. Teens listen to all types of music! The following table provides examples of artists that appeal to teens within each genre.

There are many subgenres to the categories in the table. For example, in Pop some examples of subgenres are Brit Pop, Dance Pop, Euro Pop, Latin Pop, New Wave, Pop Rap, Pop Rock, Soft Rock, Teen Pop Vocal Pop, and on and on . . .

Country Music	Dance Music	Folk Music
Allen Jackson	Madonna	Tracy Chapman
Dixie Chicks	Pink	Indigo Girls
Garth Brooks	Bobby Brown	Bob Dylan

Latin Music	Rap/Hip-Hop	Reggae/Ska
Jennifer Lopez	Eminem	Peter Tosh
Shakira	Mary J. Blige	Bob Marley
Enrique Iglesias	Missy Elliot	Shaggy
	Dr. Dre	
	P. Diddy (Sean "Puffy" Combs)	

Rock, Pop, etc.

Alternative	*Hard Rock/Heavy Metal*	
U2	Metallica	
Tori Amos	Iron Maiden	
Nirvana	Korn	

Pop	*Classic Rock*	*Christian*
Christina Aguilera	Jimi Hendrix	Petra
matchbox twenty	Santana	Jars of Clay
No Doubt	Bruce Springsteen	Amy Grant

HOW WILL I EVER KEEP UP?

There are many selection tools out there to help you become more knowledgeable about teen music, but first, you must get an idea of what music is popular with the age level you serve. Your approach in one community may not work as well as another. Take a chance! Not only does this knowledge help you build a collection, but it will also help you communicate with the teens who come into the library and the ones you mingle with while doing outreach. You may even attract teens into the library who aren't interested in books!

The first step in this process of investigation is to ask the teens in your community what kind of music they like. Visit your area high schools, middle schools, coffee bars, malls, sports events, concerts, and so on. Pay specific attention at lunchtimes and after school to what music is being played loudly in cars! You can set up a table of giveaways at any community event to support a music survey for teens.

An informal survey can be as simple as a basic question that you would ask a teen when working with them one-on-one. It may also include a follow-up question or two.

- "What do you think of MTV?"
- "Do you watch it?"
- "Do your friends watch it?"
- "What do your parents think?"

Formal and informal surveys are great methods to use to gain input from teens. An informal survey can connect you with teens without requiring that they fill out paper surveys or, more importantly, put their name to an opinion. Surveys are a great way to become familiar with your unique teen community, as well as helping you to get to know your teens individually. When you ask a teen for an opinion, you will certainly get some candid responses. This also is a way for you to become familiar with teens and learn names of frequent library users or teens who do not use the library at all.

Formal surveys can take the form of a passive program, or any way you can officially record information. An example of a passive program/survey is to ask teens where they like to purchase the music to which they listen. (See Figure 4.1.) You can then have a drawing for the participants and give the winners the gift cards they preferred. This also helps you gain ideas for prizes for your teens that they want, and you will

Figure 4.1
Sample Passive Program Survey: Where? Do You Buy? Your CDs?

Where?
Do You Buy?
Your CDs?

If you were going to win a gift card to buy a new CD, at which store would you prefer

to be able to use the gift card? (Choose only one.)

Tower Records

Virgin Records

Wal-Mart

Target

Best Buy

Circuit City

Complete the following for a chance to win a CD Gift Card:

Name: _____   Age: _____ Grade: _____

School: _____

E-mail: _____   Phone: _____

lead to greater participation in your programs. This type of informal survey is great to take into classrooms or to spark interest at community events. A drawing for CDs or fast food gift certificates to local music stores is the perfect way to show teens that you want to know their music opinions!

Remember

Don't limit yourself to just asking or surveying the teens who visit your library. You won't have a true sample of teens' opinions if you do!

It is vital that you listen to local radio stations. Radio is the most important resource for music knowledge available to teen librarians, but it is often ignored. Teen librarians should listen to at least one half-hour of "teen radio" a day. If you have a long commute, you can always listen in your car. If not, why not have a listening station in your library or have a Discman/radio or small stereo at work? If you can have the stereo in the teen area, this would be even better. You could get the responses on new music firsthand from teens. Knowing and selecting music is as important as choosing books for teens. Radio can help you. My advice? Just do it!

Radio station survival depends on it being in tune with teens through music, advertisements, and announcements. Radio stations must be aware of what music is important to their teenage listeners. You can discover popular music, new music, and events that are targeted to your service area just by listening a few minutes a day. Also you will become familiar and comfortable with the lyrics and music artists. Selecting music will become quick, easy and on target.

Examples of Formal Survey Questions

Have you ever visited the public library?
If you answered yes:
What CDs or types of music should the library have more of in its collection?
If you answered no:
What CDs or types of music would make you want to visit the library?
What are the top two radio stations you love to listen to?

Advertisements on the radio are also important! You can keep up-to-date with events, concerts, pop culture, and products by listening and not turning the dial. Once you have recognized the hot stations, you may even want to advertise library programs during prime time of teen listening!

An Activity to Get You Familiar With Radio . . .

Listen to at least six radio stations in your area. (Or as many as there are available!) Stretch yourself and your musical tastes. Listen to stations that appeal to teens and especially those you wouldn't normally listen to on your own. (If you follow through with the survey above, it will certainly help you identify the teen stations you should focus upon.) For each station you listen to, write down the artist or group and title of the song that is playing. As you listen, write down what you believe a teen would think of the song. Then directly ask teens to critique the same songs and see how on target you are with your thoughts. Since music is personal, one cannot group teens into specific music opinions. However, this will help you choose music for your collections and learn teens' musical tastes. This activity will work especially well if you have a large group of teens who like a particular song or artist!

Lastly, radio stations often have fabulous Web sites that have playing lists. This is a great help when you missed the title of a certain song or an artist while you were listening. Also, this is a great selection tool when purchasing music.

Movies targeted at teens usually give great exposure to musicians and groups. Keep track of the popular movies in the theatres or via rentals. Soundtracks of these movies will also be in great demand. Often these are ideal for library purchase because of the varied selections known to be on the soundtracks.

WARNING!—PARENTAL ADVISORY—EXPLICIT CONTENT

Ahhh . . . the slippery slope. There is a plethora of information about the beginnings of the parental advisory sticker. The progression of politics' "political correctness" sparked content labels for CDs. At this time there are various labels being put on CDs, and one can easily become confused. Here are the definitions of the most common CD labels:

Ways to Familiarize Yourself with Teen Music #1

Watch VH1, MTV, The Country Music Channel, and other music stations. (Don't forget to watch and listen at different times of the day.)

Parental Advisory Label

This is a label that is used on a volunteer basis by the individual record company and artist. It is a permanent label on the CD cover. The RIAA (Recording Industry Association of America) is active in promoting these labels. The mission is to notify listeners that there may be explicit language, violence, sex, or substance abuse represented on the CD. Some retail stores require the individual purchaser to be 18 or older.

Ways to Familiarize Yourself with Teen Music #2

Read *Rolling Stone*, *SPIN*, *Hit Parader*, *Billboard*, and any other popular music magazine you can get your hands upon.

Edited Version Label

When a CD has been modified from the original recording, it is considered edited. CDs can receive this Edited Version Label if the original version has a Parental Advisory Label. This CD does not include the same word-for-word recording as the original. The CDs with this label are also known as "clean" or "sanitized." Wal-Mart, K-Mart, and other retail stores will often have these available for purchase.

Edited Version Also Available Label

CDs that have the Parental Advisory Label on their "original recording" may also have an edited version available. If so, there is an additional type of label that will indicate this—Edited Version. It's important for libraries to be especially aware of this label. You may have teens or their parents asking for the "clean version," especially if the label states that one is available. Your library collection development policy should include the library's stand on "clean" CDs.

In the library, these types of labels can cause great misunderstanding. The record companies attach these labels to the CDs—the library does not. The bottom line is that the sticker is at the sole discretion of the record label. Many CDs that potentially have explicit material do not have a sticker. Some have the lyrics printed and displayed in the CD case instead. Many CDs that could be questioned have neither. Although there have been significant efforts, there is no standardization regarding this label. To make it more complicated, what may be explicit and offensive to one individual may not be to another. This can cause intense confusion when setting up a music collection.

Ways to Familiarize Yourself with Teen Music #3

Read *Seventeen*, *CosmoGirl*, *Teen People*, and the like. Popular music stars are often featured.

When making a music purchase, be aware that "clean" (or edited) versions may be available. Issues such as the following will need to be considered before you purchase certain titles.

- Do you purchase both the clean version and the original, or one or the other?
- What if you have a budget that can accommodate only one version?
- Is just having the clean version censorship?
- Is having only the original version being too focused?

This is a decision that the library must make, preferably in the collection development planning process. It cannot be stressed enough how important it is to include music in this document. It provides a clear line of what you should have in your collection if (and when) you are confronted with such confusing matters as various labels.

This all leads into the area of censorship. Because of the concept of intellectual freedom, there is a huge gray area that involves the library when it comes to music. Be sure that you are familiar with the stand of your library on challenged music. This is an issue in which it is better to be proactive instead of reactive. And remember, the parental advisory label is meant to bring awareness to the decision-making process; it is not intended to make the individual decision for you. It is vital that policies be in place to guide library staff during challenges. It is also important for a library's administration to have a clear understanding of the goals of any collection developed by the library, but especially when it comes to popular music.

How can I claim to understand the music when the lyrics cause me to have a parental flinch?

Some teen music will not fit your personal tastes. Some of it may even be repulsive or downright "nasty" to you. Some music may be too slow, or perhaps it needs to be listened to at roaring decibels and the only place you can do that is in your car. Some music may bring on a sense of anxiety or put you to sleep. Familiarity is the key. It shows a great respect to teens when you work with them that you know teen music and its trends.

Ways to Familiarize Yourself with Teen Music #4

Cruise your book and music stores. Many have listening stations for shoppers to sample new music.

Music lyrics can be found easily on the Internet. Many CD covers include lyrics. If you hear a song on the radio or on a new CD and you don't understand the lyrics, you can find them! The days of misheard lyrics do not have to exist anymore. Becoming familiar with lyrics will also help you understand the language of teens in your area. Slang and new use of words often come from music lyrics.

When a teen walks into the library and he/she requests the lyrics to a song, it will be important that you can at least feel your way around the question. Many music artists have unusual and unique ways of spelling their names. Look at radio station Web sites, cruise the music stores and bookstores, read music magazines, and ask the teens! Chances are they will be thrilled to help you, as well as start a conversation about the group. It's a good idea to keep a cheat sheet of new groups and their spellings. Share this information with your colleagues. They will appreciate it!

It's also important to know the musician's spellings because that knowledge will allow you to quickly conduct a search in the on-line catalog for items, requests, and ordering music. This often is regarded as a small detail, but it can really make or break you when working with teens.

Misspelled musical groups?

- N'Sync
- Staind
- Linkin Park

Parents Want to Know!

Imagine this scenario . . .

It's 7:00 P.M. on a Tuesday evening and you've just received an angry phone call from a parent of a teen. This mother is upset because her son checked out a CD from the library. The CD has "swear" words in several of the songs, and in another song someone's mother is being disrespected. What do you do?

Each complaint about library material is unique. There isn't one pat answer for this type of issue. There are ways to keep concerns and complaints in perspective when communicating with parents of teens. There is no denying that there are all different types of music available. This falls under the same class as the print materials available at the library. There is something for everyone.

When a parent brings a concern about music to you, there are a few things to keep in mind.

Purpose

A public library has all types of materials available for patrons. Because of this, there will always be something objectionable. If the teen librarian is knowledgeable about the music collection, it will be easier to assist the patron in finding music that is acceptable to both the teen and the parent.

Filling in the Gaps . . .

If a parent asks you for help in learning about popular teen music, this is an opportunity for you to suggest they listen to local radio stations, read popular culture–related magazines, and review other popular culture resources. Often parents are so busy that it is difficult for them to keep up with their teen's interests.

Ways to Familiarize Yourself with Teen Music #5

Listen to the radio!

Source to Help Parents

Subscribe to the publication *Plugged In* from Focus on the Family and/ or browse their Web site. This is a resource that focuses on the family view of teen popular culture and is of interest to both teens and parents. The teen music reviews are separated as follows:

- Artist
- Album
- Genre
- Chart Action
- Reviewer
- Pro-Social Content
- Objectionable Content
- Summary/Advisory

The reviews are up-to-date, and will assist you in becoming familiar with teen music. The Web site is: http://family.org/pplace/pi/music/.

Listen, Listen, Listen

Listen to parents. It is very frustrating to be a parent of a teen, especially with trends shifting almost daily. Often parents want a friendly ear, and a librarian can provide this. If you think about it, we are in the same predicament as parents as far as trying to keep up. We know how time-consuming and frustrating that can be! Listen, listen, listen.

Ways to Familiarize Yourself with Teen Music #6

Keep an eye on the Rock and Roll Hall of Fame and Museum in Cleveland! The Web site is http://www.rockhall.com.

Keep Everyone Informed

Communicate with your library administration and community. More education about the importance of music in a teen's life is vital. Each age level in the library focuses on their customer needs. Teens cannot be left out of this loop. By having this communication, you will find that welcoming teen music in your library will come with ease.

Provide Options

Once again, try to have both the original version of a CD and the clean version available, especially if your community asks for it.

GONE AGAIN?—HOW DO I KEEP CDS FROM BEING STOLEN?

Missing and stolen CDs are a fact of life in the public library. This can be very hard to swallow, especially when your budget is limited. The hard fact is that if someone wants to steal something, they will. Please keep in mind that other items in the library are prone to theft also: magazines, DVDs, newspapers, books, stock reports, CD-ROMs, comic books, graphic novels . . . oh, and don't forget, the toilet paper and towels in the public restrooms! Theft should not be used as an excuse to not have music for teens. This medium should be considered the same as all the other items in the library, with a few special considerations.

Ways to Familiarize Yourself with Teen Music #7

Watch the MTV Music Awards, Grammys, Teen Choice Awards, Latino Music Video Awards, Country Music Awards, and so on.

There are some things you can do to deter theft:

- Have some type of security strip on the CD or the case that works with your security system or gate.
- Your music collection should be out in the open. If your collection is in a corner or tucked away in the back of the library, see if you can move it. This is also helpful with marketing. If they see it, they will come!
- Mirrors deter theft. If at all possible, install mirrors in your audiovisual area.
- Librarians need to be moving. Too often it's acceptable for the librarian to sit at her/his desk looking at the computer with great abandon. If library employees are helping patrons and are visible, it's harder to steal materials.
- Replace stolen CDs! Are you asking to have them stolen again? Maybe. However, your teen patrons who will return the CDs should not be punished by the theft of others.
- Establish a similar loan period for CDs to what is in place for books. Some libraries only have one-week checkout for CDs. Give the teen patrons time to listen to the CD! Three weeks is the ideal.
- Don't be surprised if CDs that are considered missing are returned on your desk. Often, materials are returned to the library without ever being checked out! Be glad you got them back.
- Have an amnesty day or week for teens. Forgive fines for overdue materials. You will find your teen library users increase. Teens who have fines that keep them from checking out materials will be able to do so again. Speak to your administration about this—it is also a great public relations move during national library week or other special events.

Ways to Familiarize Yourself with Teen Music #8

Keep track of popular songs used in teen television programs. Often at the end of an episode, the cover of the CD with acknowledgments to the songs and artists are featured.

HOW DO I MAKE MY LIBRARY COLLECTION APPEALING TO TEENS?

Marketing is extremely important with your teen music collection. Often there are space limitations for storing CDs in a public library. Therefore, all areas of the library are good places to promote the teen music collection. The teen area, regardless of its location to the music area, will be the prime place to promote new artists, popular artists, and popular culture.

Ways to Familiarize Yourself with Teen Music #9

Pay close attention to top lists at the end of the year on both radio and television, as well as in popular magazines.

Seven Ideas

- Have teens prepare a bulletin board or display. Teen advisory groups would be a great place to start. Perhaps the after school crowd would be interested.

- Keep magazine issues and use the pictures or headlines for bulletin boards.

- Ask the teens to write reviews of music CDs and post them in the library.

- Place CDs with print material throughout the library. For example, put CDs by specific artists next to their biographies. If a teen magazine has a music artist on the cover, place the CDs by the magazines.

- Buy many copies of CDs that you know will be popular. This perhaps is the best marketing strategy ever. If materials can be reserved at your library, make this process easily available and easy to use. Guides are helpful because often teens want to do the selections themselves. Teens don't always know they can get on a waiting list for CDs.

- Shelve as many CDs as possible face out. The covers grab a teen's attention.
- A readily available place to shelve recently returned CDs is a surefire way to make the new and popular CDs available. Make sure this service is in an area that is visible.

A PROGRAM ON TEEN MUSIC? HELP!

Ways to Familiarize Yourself with Teen Music #10

- Read the paper, community announcements, and area music publications. These will help you learn about your local bands. Contact these groups; many times they will be willing to donate a CD in order to gain the free exposure.
- Watch television advertisements closely. Many popular songs are featured or made popular by the product.

Passive programs are a hit with teens. (A passive program is one that does not require the attendance of a teen at a particular event, or on a specific day, such as those described below.) Many teens are satisfied with and appreciate quizzes, surveys, and the like in place of having to physically attend a program at a certain time. Passive programs can include a drawing for prizes, or just finding out what teens think. Some program prizes could include gift cards, batteries (for portable music players), candy, "cool" pens, CDs, and so forth.

Here are some passive program ideas for you to use in your library

- What's your favorite lyric? (See Figure 4.2.)
- Match the misheard lyrics. (See Figure 4.3.)
- Match the high school picture with the artist.
- What musician or group recorded the following cover songs?
- Match the advertisement song with the product.
- Music quizzes.
- Award show guessing games (Grammy awards, MTV music awards, etc.).

Figure 4.2
Sample Passive Program Idea: What's Your Favorite Lyric?

You Like What?

Write down you favorite song lyrics and tell why they are your favorite…

Who is the artist who performs your favorite lyrics?

Complete the information below to enter a drawing for a free gift card from your

favorite music store:

Name: _____   Age: _____ Grade: _____

School: _____

Figure 4.3
Sample Passive Program Idea: What Did She Just Sing?

What did she just sing?

Match the misheard lyrics with the correct song and win a great prize!

_____ A. You can't always get a Chihuahua.

_____ B. . . . center of a rhododendron.

_____ C. I worship Mr. Clean.

_____ D. My love is like butter
       Green Beans are abused for being strange.

_____ E. I've got a too tight tutu and a microphone.

_____ F. It's like 10,000 phones when all you need
      is a dime.

_____ G. Parmesan, parmesan.

_____ H. Don't let the germs fly high, Listerine.

_____ I. I ate new crayons, But I threw up again.

_____ J. Gimme a meatball, gimme a meatball.

1. **ALL OVER YOU**
   By Live

2. **IRONIC**
   By Alanis Morrissette

3. **DAUGHTER**
   By Pearl Jam

4. **MACHINEHEAD**
   By Bush

5. **WHERE IT'S AT**
   By Beck

6. **TUBTHUMPING**
   By Chumbawamba

7. **BEAUTIFUL PEOPLE**
   By Marilyn Manson

8. **HOW BIZARRE**
   By OMC

9. **GLYCERINE**
   By Bush

10. **YOU CAN'T ALWAYS**
    GET WHAT YOU WANT
    By Rolling Stones

Name: _____ Age: _____ Grade: _____

School: _____

Email: _____ Phone: _____

If you prefer, here are more "active" programs to entice teens to visit the library; try one of these:

- Plan karaoke night
- Host local bands
- Provide areas for music listening
- Share your favorite music
- Present CD swaps

Ask the teens you serve what kinds of music programs would interest them. You can also ask them to help you plan and put together a program!

Ways to Familiarize Yourself with Teen Music #11

Don't forget about your teens. They know more about music than you do, so ask, ask, ask!

You don't have to know everything about teen music. Even if you know a little, you are ahead of the game! The groundwork for having a good music collection is knowledge of your patrons, their interests, and, ultimately, pop culture. You can never be too secure of music knowledge in our world of change. There will always be new groups, new styles, and new music directions to spin your teens into popular culture frenzy. All we can do as teen librarians is to give it our best shot, stay on the wave, and not forget what is important to the age level we serve.

5

TEENS AND THE BIG SCREEN: BUILDING A VIDEO COLLECTION TO BRING THEM TOGETHER

Sarah Flowers

Why should you have videos and DVDs in a public or school library collection for teens? Why not? Like other library materials, videos can be a great source of both information and entertainment. Video is a superb medium for storytelling, whether that story is a fictional one or a true one. What's more, today's teens are accustomed to getting their information from the small screen. And sometimes a picture really is worth a thousand words. Home video has been around for almost thirty years now; if your teen collection does not include videos, you are definitely living in the past.

This chapter will provide the following information on videos and DVDs in libraries for teens:

- The various types of film media
- Where and how to learn more about new titles
- How to evaluate films
- Marketing and merchandising considerations
- Costs
- Weeding
- Video distributors

Walt Crawford, columnist for *American Libraries* and a senior analyst for the Research Libraries Group, says, "Videos make awful substitutes for good books. Books make terrible substitutes for good videos. Libraries should include both, along with other media, as they serve the mission of each library" (Crawford 2002, 11).

And that is the key. What is your library's mission? If you are serving teens, you should think seriously about collecting videos and DVDs. Your library's mission will tell you what kinds of videos you want to collect.

VIDEO TYPES

The first thing most people think about when they hear the word "video" is popular feature films. There are certainly multitudes of those to choose from, and they often cost less than hardcover books. Whether your teen services budget includes money for feature films is probably a function of your library's policies. Some libraries, acknowledging that they can never compete with the local video store, simply don't collect feature films at all. Others concentrate on the "classics"—older films, films based on novels and plays, films on various "best" lists. The whole issue of feature films brings up a number of controversial issues: Can you buy a film based on a classic novel, such as the 1992 adaptation of James Fenimore Cooper's *Last of the Mohicans*, even if it is rated "R" by the MPAA? Can you buy purely entertainment films like the recently released *Spider-Man*? How about films based on more recent books, such as *Harry Potter and the Sorcerer's Stone*? How about anime? Are you required to find two positive reviews in standard sources? Does the Teen Department even have money budgeted for feature films, or does the Adult Services or Media Librarian do all video selecting? The answers to these questions will determine whether you have a feature film collection for teens at all.

The other major type of video is the non-feature, or special interest, film. This includes documentaries, educational videos, performance videos, entertainment videos, anime, and even episodes of television series. In past years, this category consisted largely of expensive independently produced documentaries and some PBS videos. Today, thanks to cable channels such as A&E (Arts & Entertainment), the History Channel, and the Discovery Channel, there are many quality non-feature videos available at reasonable prices.

FINDING OUT ABOUT AND OBTAINING VIDEOS

Video collection development follows the same principles as print collection development. Obviously you want to get the best possible films for your collection dollar. Some of your best sources for finding out which films are best are sources you are probably already using, including *Booklist*, *School Library Journal*, *Library Journal*, and *Voice of Youth Advocates (VOYA)*.

School Library Journal reviews as many as thirty videos per issue, although most are for younger children. *SLJ* lists videos in general categories such as Art, Guidance, Health, Language Arts, Science, Social Studies, and so on. It gives a recommended grade level as well as full bibliographic and purchasing information. Addresses and phone numbers of distributors are listed at the end of the Multimedia Review section.

Where Do I Learn About Videos?

The following journals contain information about new videos for teens:

- *Booklist*
- *School Library Journal*
- *Library Journal*
- *Voice of Youth Advocates (VOYA)*
- *Video Librarian*

Booklist puts all video reviews in the Media section, but has subcategories for Adult and Youth videos. If you are purchasing for high school age patrons, be sure to read the Adult reviews as well as the Youth section. *Booklist* normally reviews fewer films than *SLJ*—only a dozen or so per issue—but, of course, *Booklist* is published more frequently than *SLJ*. The distributor's phone number is given in each listing.

Library Journal also reviews about a dozen non–feature films in each issue, but does not specifically review films for youth. As with *Booklist*'s Adult reviews, though, listings frequently include films that are appropriate for teens, especially high schoolers. Distributors' phone numbers, addresses, and Web site addresses are included in the bibliographic details.

Voice of Youth Advocates (VOYA) has recently started a movie review column called "Teen Screen." It now appears in the April, August, and December issues. Six to eight non–feature films are reviewed in each issue, usually with a common theme linking them. Examples of themes include body image (June 2001), music (August 2002), and extreme sports (December 2002). All films reviewed are appropriate for teens, and the listings follow *VOYA*'s Q/P (Quality/Popularity) rating system and MJS (Middle School/Junior High/Senior High) age rating system. Complete contact information for distributors is listed at the end of the column.

Video Librarian is a bimonthly magazine that exclusively reviews videos of all sorts, and for all ages. About 200 titles are reviewed in each issue. A subscription to *Video Librarian Plus* includes the print magazine as well as access to the premium features of the Web site (http://www.videolibrarian.com). Non-subscribers have access to recent video reviews on the Web site, but subscribers also have the ability to search an on-line database of over 12,000 reviews. *Video Librarian* (both print and on-line versions) also has a list of distributors, with addresses, phone numbers, and Web site addresses. Each video reviewed is rated from one to four stars and is given an audience notation: K for preschool-Kindergarten level, E for Elementary (grades 1–3), I for Intermediate (grades 4–6), J for Junior High (grades 7–8), H for High School (grades 9–12), C for Colleges and Universities, and P for Public Libraries. Some videos have multiple audience notations. Public performance rights, where available, are noted. Reviews are grouped by subject, with space reserved near the back for feature films just released in video or DVD format.

Another source of short, non-feature videos that are appropriate for teens is YALSA's Best Videos and DVDs for Young Adults lists. The list is prepared each year at the ALA Midwinter meeting. A committee of fifteen YALSA members previews videos throughout the year. They solicit videos from a large list of distributors, view them, and have teens view them. All videos for the list must have been released in the past two years, must be 60 minutes or less in length, and must have teen appeal. At the Midwinter meeting, the committee views the nominated videos in their entirety and votes whether to include each in the list. See http://www.ala.org/yalsa/booklists/video for lists of past selections, and the complete description of policy and procedures. Beginning in 2003, this list is also reproduced in the winter issue of *Young Adult Library Services*, the professional journal published by YALSA.

Each year the Selected DVDs and Videos for Young Adults Committee presents a program at the ALA Annual Meeting, at which they show clips from the selected films. This is an excellent opportunity for youth services librarians to preview some excellent videos. The list is published on YALSA's Web site, in *School Library Journal*, in *Booklist*, and in *VOYA*. Lists up to and including 2002 appear in the spring issue of *Journal of Youth Services in Libraries (JOYS)*.

If you are looking for videos on a particular topic, an excellent free resource is DocuSeek Film and Video Finder (http://www.docuseek. com). DocuSeek searches the collections of several of the major producers and distributors of documentary and educational videos, including Bullfrog Films, Direct Cinema Limited, Fanlight Productions, First Run/Icarus Films, Frameline, New Day Films, and Women Make Movies. It has an excellent search engine that allows a search by keyword, as well as by general subject, length, awards, grade level, and more.

Anime (Japanese animated stories) videos are a class unto themselves. They are seldom, if ever, reviewed in the usual library review sources. However, there are some magazines and Web sites that keep up on the anime market. *Animerica* magazine regularly reviews anime videos. The Animé Café Web site (http://www.abcb.com) includes a synopsis, a review, and a "parent's guide" for each video that indicates the recommended age range for the video.

Facets Multimedia (http://www.facets.org) produces a massive print catalog of video titles, including many international films. Their collection consists primarily of feature films, but they do have a number of documentary and educational videos as well. Each entry includes release year, director, and a synopsis of the video. The Facets catalog is one of the best sources for finding out what videos are currently in print.

The larger library book jobbers, such as Baker & Taylor and Ingram, carry videos, both feature (including anime) and non-feature. Baker & Taylor (http://www.btol.com/library.cfm) publishes "The Alert," both in print and on-line. It is similar to their paperback "Forecast" newsletter, but it is for VHS, DVD, and CD products. Baker & Taylor customers can also sign up for "e-lists" that will alert them to the latest in video. Ingram (http://ingramlibrary.com) also offers e-mail alerts for subscribers, as well as lists for their "ipage" subscribers.

The major on-line book and music stores, such as Amazon (http://www.amazon.com), Barnes & Noble (http://www.bn.com), and Suncoast video (http://www.suncoast.com) are a readily available source for many videos that are currently in print. This is especially true for feature films and anime, and for popular non-feature items such as the public television offerings. They are less helpful in the realm of the educational and independent documentary films.

Many distributors of educational and documentary films produce catalogs, which they will be happy to send to you. These catalogs vary in their usefulness to the librarian. Many, for example, are very lax about listing the copyright and release dates of their videos, so it is difficult to tell if a video is really new, or just new to this particular distributor (or not new at all). The best catalogs include thorough descriptions of the films, as well as complete bibliographic information. Many distributors now also have Web sites that include the same information. A selected and annotated list of distributors that specialize in high-quality non-feature videos, including those for teens, can be found at the end of this chapter.

Even after you have read reviews, checked the distributor's or producer's Web site, and done everything you can to investigate a video, you still may not know if it is right for you. Since many non-feature and educational videos are expensive, you may not want to buy one unless you know that it will be appropriate in your school or library. Fortunately, most distributors are willing to send preview copies of videos. You can request a title for preview by calling, e-mailing, writing, or faxing the distributor. Usually you will receive a video promptly, and will have 30–45 days to preview it. If you decide to buy it, you can simply pay the invoice that comes with the video. If you decide it is not right for you, you can return it.

EVALUATING VIDEOS

What constitutes a good video? At the ALA Midwinter Meeting in 2001, a group of teens met with the YALSA Selected DVDs and Videos for Young Adults Committee to discuss what they liked and didn't like in the videos that they see. These teens were primarily thinking about the videos they watch in school, but their comments extend to all kinds of films.

- They said that they want to see good films—films that are well-made and interesting to watch.
- They want to see films that tell a good story.
- They want to see films that don't talk down or patronize their audience, and films that don't preach to them.

These criteria are an excellent place to begin in looking for films for a teen collection. To evaluate a video, first use the same skills you have honed over years of evaluating books. The selection criteria created for YALSA's Selected Videos and DVDs for Young Adults committee is a good place to start, especially for evaluating non-feature videos. Portions of that list are given in Figure 5.1. Detailed suggestions and comments follow within the text.

Figure 5.1
Suggested Selection Criteria

A. Technical Qualities

1. Is the photography effective and imaginative?
2. Is the sound acceptable?
3. Is the editing satisfactory?
4. Do the actors have good voice quality, diction, and timing?
5. Is the acting believable and convincing?
6. Does the narrator have good voice quality, style, diction, and timing?

B. Content

1. Is it well organized?
2. Is the script well written and imaginative?
3. Is it timely or pertinent to young adult needs and interests?
4. Is the treatment appropriate for the subject?

C. Utilization

1. Will it stimulate and maintain interest?
2. Are the format, vocabulary, and concept(s) appropriate?
3. Will it affect attitudes, build appreciation, develop critical thinking, and/ or entertain?

D. Overall Effect

1. Are the technical qualities, content, and utilization combined into a pleasing whole?

Note: The YALSA Board of Directors formally approved the full list of selection criteria in July 1996 and it was amended in July 1998. It was revised by the committee in March 2000 and was again revised by the Board of Directors in July 2000.

Technical Qualities

For all videos, both feature and non-feature, technical excellence (also known as good production values) is a must. Videos with muddy sound, sloppy editing, and bad acting are not worth having in your collection.

- Is the photography effective and imaginative? The selection and handling of visuals is crucial to the success of a video project. Both live action and animated films should use color, composition, and focus effectively to present a pleasing appearance. Some so-called "educational videos" are really just slide shows. The scenes may be videotaped, but there's not much going on, and the viewer sees only a static image with some voice-over narration. This type of film will put your teen audience to sleep. Some videos consist almost exclusively of "talking heads." This approach can actually be effective, if used well. For example, in the 1999 film *Just Like Me: Talking About AIDS*, by Films for the Humanities and Sciences, six young men and women who became HIV-positive as teenagers share their individual stories. These poignant autobiographies explore the reality of contracting and living with the HIV virus. Because the film is fairly short (21 minutes), and because the young people tell their stories simply yet clearly, it works. But it is easy to misuse this technique, especially when the "talking heads" are adults who are trying to sell a point to a teen audience.

- Is the sound acceptable? Sound can be a real problem in videos, especially those that are inexpensively made. Inexplicable volume changes, problems with clarity, poor lip-synchronization, and unrealistic sound effects can mar the viewer's enjoyment of a film. Documentaries that film people in real situations are particularly prone to sound problems—without judicious editing of extraneous sounds, it can often be hard to hear the voices.

- Is the editing satisfactory? Is it clear to the viewer how scenes are connected? Do scenes flow naturally, with no jumpiness between them? Is it obvious whose point of view is being shown in each scene? For the most part, editing in films for teens should be virtually unnoticeable.

- Do the actors/narrators have good voice quality, diction, and timing? If you cannot understand the voices, you are not going to get much out of the movie. Videos that showcase real teens (not actors) must pay special attention to this aspect. If the voices are indistinct or heavily accented, subtitles should be included.

- Is the acting believable and convincing? Are the actors/narrators appealing to teens? Teens can be particularly critical about this aspect. If the acting is amateurish, overly enthusiastic, or condescending, teens will be turned off, and the video will simply become an object of derision.

Content

Evaluating content for videos is similar to evaluating content for books. Feature films parallel fiction and non-feature/documentary films parallel nonfiction.

- Is it well organized? The film should flow well from start to finish, and the intended audience should be able to follow it.

- Is the script well-written and imaginative? Almost anyone can make a movie these days, but they aren't all worth watching. The best videos, like the best books, tell a good story, whether the story is true or not. A good non-feature video should get its facts right, and should document its sources as much as possible. In videos, this is often done by using an expert to convey relevant facts or opinions. The expert should be identified by name and affiliation using on-screen titles.

- Is it timely and current? Like books, videos can age quickly. Out-of-date fashions and popular culture references stand out even more in videos than they do in books. A group of teens watching an outdated video will soon be concentrating more on making fun of the film than watching it. Also, check the copyright date on the film's closing credits as well as what is written on the box. You may find that a "new" video is in fact an older title, rereleased by a new distributor.

- Is it pertinent to young adult needs and interests? Some topics are naturals for teen interest. Others fill curriculum needs. Still others have particular local interest. This is an area where you can use your regular book selection skills to decide.

- Is the treatment appropriate for the subject? This is an area that calls for judgment on your part. In the case of animated videos, you need to decide if the animation is sophisticated enough for your teen viewers, or whether it seems too childish. Is a documentary style the right approach for a serious subject, or would a dramatized story work better? Is it free from bias or prejudice?

Usefulness

How is the video going to be used? Who is its intended audience? Is it meant to supplement the curriculum and be shown in a classroom setting, or is it a video that teens themselves will seek out in a public library? The answers to these questions determine a video's usefulness in your collection.

- Will it stimulate and maintain interest? This is going to depend a lot on the age of your audience. As with books, an older teen audience will be able to maintain interest in a documentary longer than a younger audience will. Still, it needs to keep moving and use a variety of visual techniques to keep teens interested.
- Are the format, vocabulary, and concept(s) appropriate? Silly animation for a serious subject for older teens won't work. Science and history films need to explain their background vocabulary unless they're intended for an older audience that has already studied the concepts in school.
- Will it affect attitudes, build appreciation, develop critical thinking skills, and/or entertain? Again, you have to consider your audience here. Are you buying for teachers or parents or for teens themselves? Are you buying videos to supplement curriculum, or to offer information or entertainment on subjects of interest to teens? Your own collection development standards will help you on this one.

Overall Effect

Finally, give yourself some time to consider the video's overall effect.

- Are the technical qualities, content, and utilization combined into a pleasing whole? Just like a book, a video must be seen as a complete piece of work. Teens see a lot of films, and can be very critical about them. They want to be entertained, even if the film is curriculum-based, and they don't want to be patronized. Inappropriate content or utilization and poor production values can ruin a film for teen viewing.

MARKETING AND MERCHANDISING

After you have built your video collection, what do you do with it? To begin with, how do you shelve your video collection? Much depends upon what kind of video collection you have. Generally speaking, collections of feature films are very popular and are usually shelved separately, in a high-traffic area of your library. Feature video collections need very little marketing—people find them, and they sell themselves.

Non-feature videos are another matter. There are two basic options here, with variations. The first is to shelve them as a separate video collection. The advantage to this method is that it enables users to browse the video collection easily. If you file them in Dewey (or other classification) order, subjects will be grouped together for easy access.

The second option is to interfile the non-feature videos with your nonfiction books. The advantage to this method is that materials on like subjects are shelved together—when your patron is looking for material on the planets, he or she will find the BBC/A&E production *The Planets* in 523.4, right next to books on the solar system. The disadvantage is that it makes it more difficult for users to browse for videos. Patrons who simply like to watch documentaries will find themselves wandering the aisles looking for video boxes among the books.

This last disadvantage becomes even greater when you are talking about teen collections. If your teen nonfiction is interfiled with the adult nonfiction, and you interfile videos as well, it is going to be difficult for your teen patrons to stumble on videos serendipitously. A smaller teen nonfiction collection that interfiles videos might make it somewhat easier, at least once your users are aware that the videos are there. Of course, that still leaves the problem of classifying videos as "teen" versus "adult." Many videos that are useful for curriculum-related projects as well as interesting to teens, such as NOVA programs or A&E Biography shows, are considered adult fare in most public libraries. Unless you are buying them with the Young Adult budget, they are not likely to be shelved in the teen section.

One solution to the "lost" video problem is displays. One approach is to create frequent displays on specific topics, and to include both books and videos. Another is to make occasional video-only displays, of the "See What Good Stuff We Have" sort. Yet another possibility is to have a "new video" section, similar to the "new book" section in most libraries. Keeping the new non-feature videos in a "new" display for six months or so will give your users an idea of the kinds of videos that you are buying. This can be specialized for a teen area, or simply part of the adult new book area.

Covers and Security

Consider another marketing issue—packaging of videos and DVDs. Some libraries repackage all media in dull brown or black plastic cases. This is the equivalent of covering all books with brown paper wrappers. If at all possible, use the original cover. You can accomplish this by using clear plastic cases such as "squeeze boxes" or by cutting up the original cover to use in or on another plastic case.

Security of videos can be an issue in some libraries, and this can affect how you shelve and package your videos. Clear plastic locking cases can allow the cover to be seen. If you must keep videos behind a counter, try to have the covers available for display and browsing. DVDs create additional security problems, because their size makes them easy to steal. Again, locking cases are probably your best bet to prevent theft as well as to advertise your collection. These can be purchased from a number of library supply companies such as DEMCO.

Marketing

You can market videos using the same tried-and-true methods you use for book marketing: displays, lists, newsletter articles, and even "videotalking." One simple way to market your video collection is to include videos when making pathfinder lists and other subject bibliographies. In most cases, you will not have enough titles on any particular subject to make an entire list of videos, so adding videos to other subject lists is one way to attract attention to them.

Doing small displays of videos is another good way to highlight them. It can be as simple as a small table or display rack with a dozen or so videos and a sign asking "Have you seen any of these?" A "Staff Recommendations" display can be very effective for adults. For teens, a similar display entitled "Your Friend Just Returned These" or "_____ Recommends" (insert the name of the current popular culture icon in the blank space) should work equally well. Pairing feature films with the books they are based on, or non-feature films with books on related subjects, is a great way to give your video collection a higher profile. Shakespeare plays in book form can be paired in a display with Shakespeare on video. Biography videos can be paired with written biographies, or displayed in general subject areas: musicians, sports figures, or actors.

Sports videos are a natural for teens, and there is a wide variety of types available. Besides how-to videos for every sport from baseball and soccer to snowboarding and in-line skating, there are many inexpensive videos on Olympic sports and extreme sports, such as Gravity Games and X-Games. These lend themselves easily to seasonal or other eye-catching displays, especially if you use sports equipment on your display as well.

If you collect music and concert videos, you may not have to worry about marketing—once it is known that you have them, they may rarely be on the shelves. Still, they make a popular display, especially when matched with CDs by and books about the artists. The possibilities are limited only by your imagination.

Programs

Another good way to market your teen video collection is to use them in programs. Many non-feature videos come with public performance rights, but not all do, so be sure to check before showing them to a group in the library. Of course, your program will be determined by the videos you own and the interests of your community, but here are some examples of recent videos that would be naturals for programming:

For a program for parents and teens, you could show *Tough Guise* (Media Education Foundation, 1999), or *Reviving Ophelia* (Media Education Foundation, 1998) followed by a discussion of gender roles and societal expectations. Another possibility would be a program for mothers and daughters on body image, showing all or parts of the films *Dying to Be Thin* (WGBH, 2000), *Slender Existence* (Filmaker's Library, 2000), and *The Strength to Resist: Beyond "Killing Us Softly"* (Cambridge Documentary Films, 2001).

If you have an opportunity to do a program for teachers in your local high school or middle school, you could show clips of new social studies or science films that would be useful in supplementing the curriculum. Examples could include *Figures of the Civil Rights Movement: Sit-ins and the Little Rock Nine* (Films for the Humanities and Sciences, 1999), *Daring to Resist* (a film about the young resistance members during the Holocaust by Women Make Movies, 1999), *Sunrise Over Tiananmen Square* (First Run/Icarus, 1998), and *Roller Coaster Physics*, (Discovery Communications, 2000). All of these films have been on YALSA's Selected Videos and DVDs for Young Adults lists.

For a program in a public library for teens, you will probably want to avoid the straight documentary type films, and teens have ample opportunities to see feature films, so you can concentrate on things they are unlikely to see in other venues. Showing several animated short films, such as *Village of Idiots* (1999), *The Hungry Squid* (2002), and *Black Soul* (2000), all distributed by the National Film Board of Canada, could make a good program, especially if combined with a speaker who has expertise in animation or filmmaking. Would-be zine creators might be lured to a program that includes a showing of *grrlyshow* (Women Make Movies, 2001), a film about zine-making and some of the first woman-created zines.

If you do decide to do a program with feature films, be sure that you have public performance rights. Without performance rights, a public showing of a videocassette or DVD in a public room, including a library meeting room, could be an infringement of copyright. This is true even if you do not charge a fee for the showing. You can obtain one-time rights from the movie's producer or distributor, or from a firm such as The Motion Picture Licensing Corporation (http://www.mplc.com). If you plan to show feature films on a regular basis, you will probably want to purchase a public performance site license. The Motion Picture Licensing Corporation offers an "umbrella license" that covers certain movie producers. Many major studios are represented by Movie Licensing USA (http://www.movlic.com). A site license is purchased for one year, and allows for an unlimited number of exhibitions of all movies sold for home use from the represented studios. Movie Licensing USA's site license price is based on the number of registered patrons at the library. Thus, a small library will pay considerably less than a large one will. There are discounts for systems purchasing licenses.

There are some restrictions on site or "umbrella" licenses. The license does not permit advertising the titles of movies to the general public.

That is, you can list movie titles on a poster within the library, but any advertising outside of the building can only say that you are having a "movie program." You can give general information, such as "classic screwball comedy" or "historical film" or "based on a classic novel," but you cannot list the actual titles of movies to be shown. This makes it difficult to advertise to teens unless they are already in your library. Still, if you develop a regular "Friday night at the movies" type of program, you may build up attendance over time by word of mouth, if you do a good job of selecting your films.

WEEDING

Video collections are subject to weeding rules similar to those for books. You must keep your collection fresh, or it is unlikely to circulate. Videotape deteriorates with time and use, although no one can say exactly how long a particular tape might last. Stored properly and handled appropriately, tapes can last for decades, but library patrons rarely can be troubled to treat tapes with care. "Industry experts have predicted that videotapes and other tape-based media have a life span of about 15 years, or 250 plays, depending on environmental and use factors. After that, the tape will deteriorate, losing the coating that holds the electromagnetic information" (Vollman-Grone 2002, 31).

DVDs theoretically have a longer life, but they are still new, and the experts who make the predictions probably don't realize how hard public library patrons can be on materials. There is some anecdotal evidence to indicate that DVDs may not last as long as videos in a public library setting. A commercial disc cleaning and repair device can help keep DVDs in circulation longer.

In any case, videos, like books, can lose their freshness, so weeding is essential. You defeat the purpose of selecting timely, current videos if you keep the old, tired ones on your shelves. Outdated information, especially in health and science related videos, should always be replaced with current information. The same criteria you use for weeding nonfiction books will apply to weeding non-feature videos. Feature videos usually weed themselves: they circulate until they fall apart, so you discard them, or else they stop circulating at all, so you discard them. Both feature and non-feature films can go out of print, although they also get re-released, so it is worth it to keep checking. Feature films frequently get re-released, especially on DVD, newly remastered, or with new features added.

A NOTE ON COST

The issue of cost almost always rears its head in any discussion of video in libraries. This has become a moot point in regard to feature films. Most of those are available at a cost comparable to that of books. DVDs especially tend to be released at "sell-through" prices. Non-feature videos are another case entirely. While many videos, such as the ones that derive from public or cable television programs, are available at easily affordable prices (under $40), there are still many independently produced documentaries and educational videos that cost over $100 each, sometimes as much as $200 or $300. When your budget is already tight, it is hard to justify spending that kind of money on a single film. The reason these videos cost so much is mostly a function of supply and demand. It costs money to produce and distribute movies, and the market for non-feature films is relatively small, especially compared to that for feature films, or even for nonfiction books. Additionally, many video producers are small operations, without the larger corporate umbrella (like PBS) to absorb costs. Thus, the cost is passed on to the consumer. If you are a member of a large system or a consortium, it may be possible to buy one or two copies of at least the award-winning titles, so that you can have the opportunity to share them with your patrons. If you buy one copy of an expensive film, and several libraries use it in programs that then bring teachers or parents or teens into your library for other things, then the price may be justified.

The good news is that prices for non-feature videos appear to be on the way down. The Internet has helped widen the market for these videos. Producers and distributors can reach a wider audience with their catalogs, and can advertise much more inexpensively. Additionally, according to Debra Franco, author of *Alternative Visions: Distributing Independent Media in a Home Video World*, "Increasing awareness in the public library market for non-fiction and educational videos and DVDs can have a real impact on widening the sales universe for these programs. The hope of many in the field is that the sales average for non-fiction videos and DVDs made for the educational market may rise . . . allowing prices to come down to the $50 range as an average unit price" (Franco 2002, 319).

VIDEO DISTRIBUTORS

The following is a list of distributors who frequently have films that are suitable for teen audiences. It is not a comprehensive list, by any means, but if you are looking for good independently produced films, it is a good place to start. Check out their Web sites, or send for catalogs.

A&E Home Video
19 Gregory Drive
Burlington, VT 05403
Phone: (800) 423-1212
http://www.aande.com

Sells videos and DVDs from the A&E Network and the History Channel, including the Biography series, cult TV, classic TV, and performance videos.

AIMS Multimedia
9710 DeSoto Avenue
Chatsworth, CA 91311
Phone: (800) 367-2467
http://www.aimsmultimedia.com

Offers social studies, health and guidance, science and math, language arts, the Teen Files series, and others.

Bullfrog Films
P.O. Box 149
Oley, PA 19547
Phone: (800) 543-3764
http://bullfrogfilms.com

Focuses on environmental issues and global politics, but includes a wide variety of films for young people on all topics.

California Newsreel
149 Ninth Street, #420
San Francisco, CA 94103
Phone: (415) 621-6196
http://www.newsreel.org

Includes a large collection of films on media and on African-American culture.

Castle Works/In the Mix
114 E. 32nd Street, Suite 905
New York, NY 10001
Phone: (800) 597-9448
http://www.pbs.org/inthemix

Episodes of the PBS program for teens and produced by teens. Episodes usually deal with teen-related issues from money to smoking to violence.

Cinema Guild
1697 Broadway, Suite 506
New York, NY 10019
Phone: (800) 723-5522
http://www.cinemaguild.com

A large variety of feature and non-feature films produced by independent filmmakers, often focusing on social and political issues.

Direct Cinema, Ltd.
P.O. Box 1333
Santa Monica, CA 94010
Phone: (800) 525-0000
http://www.directcinema.com

Provides a collection of short films and documentaries representing independent filmmakers—including award-winning films. Web site offers separate search options for home use and public performance videos, and searching by category, as well as keyword.

Discovery Channel School
P.O. Box 6027
Florence, KY 41002-6027
Phone: (888) 892-3484
http://www.discoveryschool.com

Discovery offers animal, science, and history films for young people.

Facets
1517 West Fullerton Avenue
Chicago, IL 60614
Phone: (800) 331-6197
http://www.facets.org

An enormous catalog of both feature and non-feature films that includes many international films.

Fanlight Productions
22-D Hollywood Avenue
Hohokus, NJ 07423
Phone: (800) 937-4113
http://www.fanlight.com

With a focus on health videos, Fanlight includes films on topics such as family, gender and sexuality, and mental health.

Filmakers Library
124 East 40th Street, Suite 901
New York, NY 10016
Phone: (212) 808-4980
http://www.filmakers.com

Documentary films on subjects including gender, multicultural studies and women's issues.

Films for the Humanities & Sciences
P.O. Box 2053
Princeton, NJ 08543-2053
Phone: (800) 257-5126
http://www.films.com

These tend to be films aimed at educating, showing all sides of an issue. They carry a number of films on political and historical topics, as well as those on social issues.

First Run/Icarus Films
32 Court Street, 21st Floor
Brooklyn, NY 11201
Phone: (800) 876-1710
http://www.frif.com

Heavily international in nature, First Run/Icarus features a variety of independent filmmakers on topics ranging from war to women's issues.

Frameline Distribution
346 Ninth Street
San Francisco, CA 94103
Phone: (415) 703-8650
http://www.frameline.org

Frameline's "mission is to support, develop, and promote lesbian, gay, bisexual, transgender, and queer visibility through media arts." Their collection includes documentaries, short features, and narratives.

Goldhil Video
137 E. Thousand Oaks Boulevard, #207
Thousand Oaks, CA 91360
Phone: (800) 250-8760
http://www.goldhil.com

Goldhil distributes hundreds of general interest videos on topics ranging from history to trout fishing.

Media Education Foundation
26 Center Street
Northampton, MA 01060
Phone: (800) 897-0089
http://www.mediaed.org

The Media Education Foundation is dedicated to promoting "media literacy." Thus, their catalog consists mainly of items related to the mass media, gender, race, commercialism, and society.

National Film Board of Canada
22-D Hollywood Avenue
Hohokus, NJ 07423
Phone: (800) 542-2164
http://www.nfb.ca

NFB carries a broad range of films. Besides films relating to Canadian history and culture, they are one of the biggest supporters of cutting-edge animation.

New Day Films
22-D Hollywood Avenue
Hohokus, NJ 07423
Phone: (888) 367-9154
http://www.newday.com

New Day is a cooperative of independent filmmakers "dedicated to bringing high quality social issue media" to their audiences. Their films often deal with social issues of interest to teens and adults.

NEWIST/CESA #7
IS 1040
UW-Green Bay
Green Bay, WI 54311
Phone: (800) 633-7445
http://www.uwgb.edu/newist

Films available are specifically for teens and deal with current social issues.

PBS Video
1320 Braddock Place
Alexandria, VA 22313
Phone: (800) 344-3337
http://www.pbs.org

Distributors of a vast array of programs aired on PBS stations, including single programs and series.

UC Berkeley Extension Media
2000 Center Street, 4th Floor
Berkeley, CA 94704
Phone: (510) 642-0460
http://ucmedia.berkeley.edu

UCEM offers educational and documentary films on a variety of topics.

WGBH Boston Video
P.O. Box 2284
South Burlington, VT 05407-2284
Phone: (800) 949-8670
http://www.wgbh.org

Producers and distributors of many PBS programs, including the NOVA and National Geographic series.

Women Make Movies
462 Broadway, Suite 500D
New York, NY 10013
Phone: (212) 925-0606
http://www.wmm.com

Videos by and about women, in the broadest possible sense.

REFERENCE LIST

Crawford Walt. " 'Watch This, It's Good For You': Thoughts on Video and Libraries." In *Video Collection Development in Multi-Type Libraries: A Handbook.* 2nd ed. edited by Gary Handman. Westport, CT: Greenwood Press, 2002.

Franco, Debra. "A Primer on the Home Video Market." In *Video Collection Development in Multi-Type Libraries: A Handbook.* 2nd ed. edited by Gary Handman. Westport, CT: Greenwood Press, 2002.

Vollman-Grone, Michael. "Public Library Video Collections." In *Video Collection Development in Multi-Type Libraries: A Handbook.* 2nd ed. edited by Gary Handman. Westport, CT: Greenwood Press, 2002.

6

NOTHING BUT NET: A VIRTUAL COLLECTION YOUNG ADULTS WILL WANT TO USE

Tracey A. Firestone

Creating a Web site to specifically address the needs of teen patrons is a wonderful addition to any young adult collection. Web collections can be built for free, although your site can be enhanced with specialty resources, such as subscription databases and other electronic resources, or by hiring professional Web developers. The Web is often considered to have nearly limitless space available for people to use. Because most young adult librarians are accustomed to working within the very narrow space limitations in their physical collections, many embrace the possibilities of the Web. Creating an on-line collection is a chance to put *everything* that could appeal to teens in one place. Well-developed and well-maintained on-line collections can often reach patrons who cannot (or simply will not) enter your doors. On the other hand, poorly developed sites with out-of-date links can discourage users from returning to your site, and will only reinforce the myth that libraries are dusty old places that have not kept up with the times. Simply put, having a bad site can be worse than having no on-line presence at all.

This chapter will provide the following information on building an on-line collection for teens:

- Definitions of related terms
- Advantages and challenges

- Preliminary work to help prepare for building the collection (site layout, design, navigation, accessibility, etc.)
- Developing content
- Reviewing and revising the site
- Promoting the collection
- Maintenance
- Sources for use in developing the collection
- Suggested on-line resources for use in your site

Developing an on-line collection does have one aspect that is unique to the medium; you can control and manipulate the appearance of the collection. Even in situations where you are "stuck" using your library's overall Web appearance, you have the capability of manipulating the wording used on the page and the overall selection of links provided to clearly address the needs of your teenage population.

To make things easier, the following terminology will be used as it's described below within the scope of this chapter, although these words are often used interchangeably elsewhere:

- **On-line Collection (OC)**—a collection of materials that is accessible on-line but includes various electronic resources. Collections can include Web pages/sites, subscription databases, your library's on-line catalog, and access to e-books and informational content (that may or may not be available elsewhere).
- **Web Collection (WC)**—a collection of links, restricted to Web pages/sites only.
- **Web Page (WP)**—a single page of information available on the World Wide Web (for example—the YALSA page that describes the Printz Award is a Web page, http://www.ala.org/yalsa/printz/index.html).
- **Web Site (WS)**—a collection of pages created and maintained under one name (for example—the YALSA site, http://www.ala.org/yalsa/, which contains the Printz Award page, as well as dozens of other informational pages).

There is no single "right" way to develop an on-line collection that will be perfect for every library. Your job is to find which "right" way will be best for you, your library, and most of all, your patrons. This chapter will discuss many of the important issues and areas of consideration you must address when creating or updating your library's teen page/site.

ADVANTAGES, CHALLENGES, AND CONSIDERATIONS

Many of the advantages you will find in having an on-line collection can also create challenges. None of these challenges should dissuade you from creating the collection, but you should be aware of them, as well as some possible solutions.

Advantages of an On-line Collection:

- The Web is always available to your patrons
- Your teen patrons can access sites from around the world
- Virtually limitless space
- Easier to assist teens with sensitive subjects
- Teens are basically "free" from age discrimination while using the Web
- Updating a Web page is relatively easy

Advantage: The Web is available to your patrons 24 hours a day, 7 days per week, and 365 days per year.

Challenge: Your patrons can access the materials available at their convenience, but the professional support that is available in a physical library, or even on-line via e-mail or on-line chats, is not. Patrons who do not find their answers are more likely to walk away and never ask (in person or via e-mail) how to find the answer to their question.

Consideration: Provide ample opportunities for patrons to send e-mail comments and follow-up questions. Be sure to always write out your full e-mail address for users who must go to another e-mail interface to send messages.

24/7 in Your Future?

Many libraries have developed 24 hours a day—7 days a week reference services. The Clevnet Library Consortium in northeast Ohio offers such a service. Although not limited to teens, its 24/7 homework is designed for students and can be accessed at http://www.homeworknow.net/

Advantage: When in an on-line environment, your patrons can access sites from all over the globe.

Challenge: Patrons of all ages, from all over the globe can access your site too. This can create difficulties if on-line databases or other services are available only to residents or cardholders.

Consideration: If a particular service is available only to your library's cardholders or local residents, be sure to make that clear.

Advantage: On-line collections are known for having virtually limitless space.

Challenge: Limitless space can be used to create limitless subdivisions and subcategories of information; but in actuality, these may only clutter up your site and make it difficult to navigate.

Consideration: Build your Web site with the "three click rule" in mind. For years the standard has been that users should be able to access whatever they need within three clicks after entering your site.

Advantage: When using an on-line collection, there is no face-to-face contact, so it is easier to investigate sensitive subjects.

Challenge: The Internet is a vast collection of reputable resources mixed among some of the most inaccurate and misleading information available. Patrons might not find answers to their questions due to faulty search strategies. They also might discover erroneous information that, with many sensitive subjects, could leave them in physical or emotional jeopardy.

Consideration: Provide links to good sources of information on the kind of sensitive subjects teens might be looking to explore. In addition, provide ample opportunity for teens to e-mail questions to the library. Be sure to note that questions can be sent "anonymously."

Advantage: Teens like the Web because they are free from age discrimination and can "go" anywhere they want with a simple click of the mouse.

Challenge: Teens like the Web, sometimes to the point of refusing to use print resources!

Consideration: Consider creating and using banners and pop-up window "ads" for services and resources that can be accessed only in the physical library. Use them on your site, and offer them to local organizations and clubs who might want to advertise the library and library services on their sites.

Advantage: Updating a Web page can be done relatively easily and as often as you want.

Challenge: It is more time-consuming to keep a site up-to-date than it is to create one.

Consideration: Reserve a set period of time on a regular, ongoing basis to make all the changes you need to make. Create folders (paper and electronic) where you can collect materials and URLs that should be considered for addition to your site.

PRELIMINARY WORK

Make Assessments

Now is the time to decide how much time you'll be able to devote to this project. First, consider how much time you have for the development of the site and for ongoing maintenance once the site is up and running. The more "stuff" you want to include on a site, the more likely that site will need regular updating. It is terribly frustrating for a user to find a huge, "well-stocked" site, only to discover the links are "broken" and the information is out of date. Chances are good that the user will leave your site and never come back. It is better to start small and have a manageable site that you are sure can be kept current.

Another very important point to consider is the ability of the person doing the physical creation and maintenance of the site. If you are on your own, you must be very honest with yourself as to what you are capable of doing and where you can go for help or guidance. Creating and developing a site is a wonderful opportunity for you to stretch your wings in a different arena, but be sure you're not adding features to your site, just to try a new technique—and be sure you're not taking on more than you can handle. If you are working with someone else, a coworker or professional Web consultant, you must know what their abilities are and try, whenever possible, to include them in your planning process.

No matter who's "making" the site, you need to know what policy limitations you must work within (for instance, some libraries are encouraged to avoid linking to commercial [.com] sites). You should also be aware of any hardware constraints you have that might inhibit some of your ideas.

The last area for assessment is potential components of content. Make a list of all the wonderful resources you'd like to see in your site. Be free to list everything that pops into your mind; include the things you know you can do, the things you think are beyond your ability, and even the things you're not sure can be done in an on-line environment. Take this list and rank the elements in order of importance. When the time comes (and it always does) to scale back your idealized version of the site, this list will make it easier to distinguish the necessary elements from the "extras."

Define Your Site

What kind of site are you creating? What is its purpose? A successful on-line collection can include information on any number of topics, but you must define for yourself and your library's patrons exactly what your collection is developed to do. Is this site to be a virtual library where users can utilize as many library services and resources as is possible, or is your site more of an advertising vehicle, where you would want to focus more on announcing upcoming programs and other library information that would entice users to visit your library in person? Are you focusing on homework needs, recreational interests, or a combination of both? Your well-planned focus for the site will make content selection an easier process.

You must also define who your audience is and what they would come to your site expecting to find. Including public school assignments is great, but do you have a population of homeschooled teens or young adults enrolled in private schools who may have vastly different research needs? Do you anticipate parents using this site to help their teens with homework questions or just to find "good" and "safe" sites for their teenaged children to visit for fun? Consider what these users would come to find on your site and what information you want to provide for them. Library Web pages can and should be used as a supplement to the library collection, but they can and will be used independently of your physical facility.

Decide what can be done with the time available, and mourn for everything you simply cannot do at this time. Be sure to keep a list of all the things you would want to do with your site if you could. These notes can be useful when you're ready to expand the site.

Plan the Layout and Navigation

Consider the kind of organizational structure you'd like to use for your site. It might not be possible to decide at this point exactly how the pages will connect to one another, but if you have an idea of the overall flow of information and the major areas of information you want to include, it can help you in your overall selection of items to include.

Writing out an outline of your site structure can make it easier to see what goes where. A traditional outline organizes the information, but only in a linear procession of facts. Using a pictorial flowchart can help you see how things can interconnect.

Try to think of a library's Web site as being much like a library's building. It must have rooms (pages) and space for everything, but it must be arranged in such a way that the public can come in and find everything they need or, at least, easily locate some way to ask for what they want.

Important Note

A basic rule of thumb for Web design is described as a three-click rule, wherein all the information on your site should be accessible within three clicks of the mouse.

A basic rule of thumb for Web design is described as a three-click rule, wherein all the information on your site should be accessible within three clicks of the mouse. Of course there are exceptions, but you should keep this concept in mind as you build your site. An easy way to make sure a patron can find what they are looking for is to include a site map, which is a separate page containing an index listing and connecting back to all of the pages in your site.

Design Your Site

Once you have an idea of what will go into your site, you need to consider how the site should appear. Design is an area where you can be creative and expressive. It's fun, and many people put a lot of time and effort into making their site look good—*but it is the content that will keep users coming back for more.*

One of the most important considerations is the Internet connection speed of the average user. As a rule, the faster a Web page loads, the better. There is, however, a significant trade-off with this approach: high-quality graphic files are usually large, and take some time to render in the user's browser. Users are not likely to be very patient with pages that take too long to display.

There should be no doubt in a user's mind as to where he or she is on the Web. Your site is probably a subsection within the overall library site, and your patrons should know that they're at the library. Consistency in a site's overall appearance is very important, but that's not to say that your site should be indistinguishable from other library department pages. Optimally, your teen site should have something (a standard navigation bar, color scheme, background, or font) that visually connects your site to the rest of the library, but also have some consistent visual cue to identify when they are in the teen section of the site.

There also should be little doubt in a user's mind about where he or she is going when he or she leaves your site to follow a link you have provided. Use descriptive titles for your links and be sure to annotate your links whenever possible. If the title describes the resource perfectly, then annotate by highlighting a particular feature or aspect of the site.

When adding subscription products, don't feel you have to use the product name in the title (although it is useful to include it in the annotation) if the title won't tell users what the product does. For example, Gale Group has wonderful on-line products, some of which library professionals would recognize by title, but to have a link for "Gale's SIRS Researcher" makes teens ask who Gale is, and what she knows about their assignment. Using a more descriptive title with an annotation such as, "Articles on Current Topics: Full-text Articles from Gale's SIRS Researcher" is more user-friendly and can help a user avoid any unnecessary duplication of research.

Accessibility Issues

Making sure that all of your patrons can access the information you have available on-line is something you must consider at all levels of development, but it is in the design of a page that many of the mistakes are made. Most of the discussion in regard to accessibility issues concerns users who are disabled, but be aware that an accessible site can be alternatively defined as one that can also be accessed via handheld devices and cell phones.

Keep in mind these issues when designing a Web page to insure that it is accessible for ALL of your teen patrons:

- Color
- Images
- Frames

Accessibility issues include everything from the colors used on a page to the use of alternative text fields for describing images. This is a subject that can be only summarized here, but there are many other resources that can provide more detailed information. Some of the on-line resources will even check your site for accessibility blockers. (See Bobby, the Lynx Viewer and the Web Accessibility Initiative in the on-line resources section for more information.)

Color

The Web allows for all the funky colors that most young adult librarians love, but your patrons may not. Remember that reds and greens are difficult for some people who are colorblind; and black backgrounds can make it difficult to get good contrast between the text and background. Use color as an accent to highlight links, but try to avoid it in any body of text to highlight words that could just as easily be bold or italicized for emphasis. Underlining should be reserved *only* for identifying hypertext links.

Images

When adding an image to your Web page, there is an optional field available for use to attach a description to the image. When this field, the "alt text" field, is left blank, users who are seeing the page through a text-only browser or hearing the page read by a computerized screen reader will only see or hear the word "image" in place of the intended image. Therefore, describe all visuals in the "alt text" field, even if you're using the image for decoration.

Frames

In Internet terminology, the term "frames" means the use of multiple, independently controllable sections on a particular Web site. Frames allow you to place a lot of information on a single page, and each "section" can be updated independently; but frames can also cause difficulty in printing, viewing, and navigation for all users—not just those with physical disabilities. Screen readers cannot easily identify the limits of the frame, so readers often read in straight lines across all frames on the screen. This can leave the user with three (or more) separate sections of information coming at them—all blended together into one very confusing document. Simply put, limit your use of frames whenever possible.

"CORE COLLECTION" CONTENT

Your site can include information as varied as library information, homework help, and recreational needs.

Library Information

Though basic library information may appear on other areas of your library's site, you want to be sure that anyone exploring your teen pages has easy access to information such as hours, directions, card application procedures, and borrowing policies. If you are reformatting this information to fit in your site, you can take the time and effort to note any teen-specific details, and explain them in teen friendly language. Having your teen programs described (and possibly even accessed) on your site can help in promotion and participation.

A library information page is a good place to put "ads" for specialized in-house services and details about any special "temporary reference" collections or pathfinders you have created to deal with class assignments.

The library information area is also the perfect place to include some kind of contact information. Contact information should include the library's complete name, address, and phone number. Remember to include an area code for out-of-town visitors to your site who might have reason to speak with you. Contact information should also include the site's main URL and an e-mail address.

A notation of who the young adult librarian is (a photo would be an added bonus) can be useful, along with information on how to locate this staff person. This is particularly nice to offer if you are concerned about teens coming in contact with staff members who are not as teen friendly as you might wish; but even in the friendliest of atmospheres, having a specific name and a face to look for can help create a sense of connection between you and the teen. Please keep in mind, however, that the security and safety of individual staff members is of the utmost importance. If there is reluctance on the behalf of an individual or other safety-related issues in a particular location, or similar concerns, this contact information may not be advisable.

Homework Help

Teens all have important and demanding jobs. For most teens, their job is to go to school and learn how to be productive members of the community. But just as adults sometimes dislike the tasks their bosses have them complete, teens are not always thrilled with the assignments they are assigned.

By including on-line resources to assist a student trying to do her homework, you are saying, "I recognize you and your informational needs, and I'm here to help." Create Webographies for the annual assignment topics you know students will need and group them by general class type (English, Science, Health), but make sure to include an alphabetic list in your site index of all the topics you've covered. Your homework help site can be enhanced with access to subscription products or services that help make the library a more valuable resource for your users than Yahoo! or AOL.

Community Information

If your community has any teen resources or organizations, your Web site offers you a great place to list them. Even for groups who do not have a Web presence, just listing the name, address, and phone numbers can be helpful to your patrons. Listing organizations and groups (such as teen drop-in centers and sports organizations) or notations about special "teen" hours at the local dance club or bowling alley can also be useful for teens and parents. These links help to connect the library to the rest of the world. Also, having links to Web sites of local organizations is a nice lead-in for requesting a reciprocal link from them to you.

Recreational Interests

Teens have a wide range of recreational interests and hobbies, and your site should recognize that fact, but it is close to impossible to include *everything* that is of interest to teens. Select a few areas of interest to highlight, trying to hit a variety of topics that might appeal to different teens. At the very least, put together a source for connecting teens to information on basic fun subjects like sports, music, television, and movies. Include local information whenever possible. Does your local movie theater have a Web page of its own? How about the popular radio stations? You can add subcategories later, but recognize that popular interests change with the wind and today's hot topic is tomorrow's joke.

Links

Finding great sites to include on your own site is one of your fun tasks when creating your Web site. Good sites can be found in many places. To help you organize your time, create folders (print and electronic) where you can store all the slips of paper with odd URLs written down, copies of e-mail messages that include useful sites, and any other ads for products or sites you want to examine.

Some of the greatest ideas for links can be found on the teen Web pages of other public libraries. See which sites are used over and over—those can comprise your initial list of sites to consider. Take the time to look at all the sites another library links to—you might find good resources that would apply to the topics you're covering in your site. If you find a great site on a topic you are not yet covering, take down the information and file it in your folder. When you do expand your site, you'll have a good place to start.

Professional journals can be used to find good sites just as they can be used to find good books. Even general-interest magazines and newspapers are adding Web site references to their articles. The reviews of Web sites are few in number and often are not created specifically for a teen's needs, but again, they can give you a place to start. Don't forget the teen magazines! They, in particular, can help you develop your section dealing with recreational interests.

You can use your workstation as a gathering place for sites that you and your colleagues discover in the course of doing your day-to-day work at the reference desk. As you work with teen patrons, create subject-specific folders within your favorites/bookmarks file. You can group topics by their general class subject and add subfolders for specific assignments. These files can easily be turned into Webographies once you see that most students who ask about a particular assignment can be helped with the resources you have collected.

Once you have long lists of great sites, cut that list down to the fewest number possible, including only the very best of what you've found. Giving your patrons a few great sites is much better than giving them the overwhelming challenge of having to sift through all that you provide to find what they need. We cannot compete with search engines, and we should not try to compete with them. Libraries are in the business of selection. In the physical library we select the books that go on our shelves, and patrons who want more than we offer will ask for interlibrary loans or go to a bookstore. If your patron wants "everything" available on a subject when they're on-line, they can use a search engine; but when they come to you and access a subject-specific Webography, you are providing an assurance of quality in the sites you've examined and have chosen to include.

Lastly, don't forget that your users have their own favorite sites. Seek "sites to consider" (remember to add an e-mail link or a form for easily submitting sites) and give patrons an opportunity to make those suggestions. Even if you choose not to use a specific site that is submitted, you might be shown where there are gaps in your collection. With that awareness in mind, you can then take the time to find resources that you would feel comfortable adding to your collection.

ON-LINE PROGRAMMING IDEAS

The Internet has opened up whole new avenues for communication in our programming world. Through your Web site, you can interact with your teens in a timely manner, but at your (and your teens') convenience. Some of the various activities and programs are described below.

E-mail

Use e-mail for program reminders. E-mail is much easier (and cheaper) than a postcard or even a telephone reminder. E-mail allows for you to easily respond to the patron unless the user takes steps to make their message "anonymous."

Forms

Adding forms to your Web site can allow teens to communicate with you electronically but without the need for the teen to use an e-mail account. Create forms with specific questions (fields) that require a response before the form will be processed (even though you cannot require that anyone give the correct information). Forms do not allow for responses, unless the user provides contact information.

You can create programs that exist only on-line, or you can incorporate on-line interaction into your traditional programs. Advertise your programs on the Web and give teens an opportunity to register with the click of the mouse. If you're concerned about out-of-district teens registering, include a space for the inclusion of a library card number.

In all registration forms, be sure to include a space to add participants' e-mail addresses. Then, after the program has been held, use your e-mail list to send out program evaluation forms. There might be a greater sense of honesty in the results if you and the program leader aren't standing there, waiting to get instant feedback. Also, for educational workshops where handouts are distributed, consider adding some of the useful content to your site after the program is held. This works well with programs you might wish to run again. You can entice young adults by taking the following approach: "This is just some of what you can get at this workshop." Free samples work well for pushing most products, including workshops.

Book Discussion

A book discussion can include several on-line components. Teens can suggest books to read through a basic form or e-mail link. An on-line vote for the next book to be read allows you to choose the titles offered, but gives the teens the final say in what they will discuss. In addition, teens could send comments electronically before the discussion is held, and these comments could be used to guide the actual discussion. After the program is held, post the comments on your side under the heading "Read what teens have to say about the books we've discussed." If you plan to use names with the teen comments on your Web site, you may need written permission from the teens or their parents. Make sure you are aware of your library's policy in this regard.

Summer Reading Program

Your summer reading program can also be enhanced with on-line participation. Registration can easily be done on-line, and book reviews could be sent to you electronically. If you hold raffles or other contests, display the prizes on your summer reading program's page beforehand and post the winners' names afterward. If you receive book reviews as a component of your summer program, post the reviews as suggestions (or warnings) for other teens. Always give the teens the option of posting them anonymously or under a pen name.

Teen Advisory Board

A teen advisory board can be expanded to include virtual members. Virtual Members can offer suggestions for consideration or topics for discussion at the next (physical) meeting. Even if you don't formally integrate the on-line participation into the board itself, you can offer the comments received via the Web for the board's consideration. In addition, the suggestions received may include issues that teens are comfortable raising only with the anonymity the Web provides.

Writer's Group

Creating an on-line extension for a writer's group gives teens an opportunity to share their work with their peers. If you have a creative writing workshop, follow up by offering participants an opportunity to post a short story or poem. Again, you might wish to give the option of posting anonymously or under a pen name. In addition, writing submissions can be solicited via the Web. You might be surprised to get postings from teens in many different areas.

In short, be creative! Teens who are virtual library users, as well as teens who might not have the time to go to library programs during "normal business hours," can participate on-line at the times that are convenient for them and only to the extent to which they are comfortable.

PREVIEW, REVIEW, AND REVISE

Before putting your page "live" on the Web, make sure you preview it using different browsers (Internet Explorer, Netscape, and Lynx), and examine the layout with the browser window open to different sizes. Try changing your browser's text size setting. Notice how the page displays under different technical circumstances.

After working on a project for a period of time, you might find yourself blind to potential problems or difficulties in navigation. Take the time to seek feedback. Show the site to people who have had nothing to do with its creation, and be sure to let them know you really do want to hear constructive criticism and any suggestions they have for making it a better site. Most people are aware of how much work and effort goes into building a Web site, so unless they are told it's OK to make critical comments they might very well hold back telling you the little things you need to hear in order to make this the best site it can be.

Ask other staff members if they feel they could use your site to help serve teen patrons' needs. Ask your friends outside of the library world to look at the site and see if "regular" adults could successfully use the site. Once you're convinced the site couldn't get any better, offer a "Teen Web Site Preview and Review" program for the teens in your community and brace yourself for the comments to come.

Take all the comments and suggestions you receive and go back to work. You shouldn't feel obligated to implement every suggestion offered, but if you have several comments about the same problem you should consider ways of changing things to improve the overall access and usability.

ADVERTISE

Once you have a site that is ready to go "live," promote it. Here are some simple tips that can help.

Send print and e-mail notices to local schools, businesses, and organizations that work for or with teens. Let them know about your new site and highlight some of the great resources that can be found. Ask them to consider adding a link from their site to yours. Be sure to include the address of your site in all of your promotional materials.

Also, once your site is live, you will get requests from other Web developers who want to link to your site (or to individual pages within your site). There is no way to prevent anyone from creating a link to your page, but you could add a notation to your contact information which states any special wording you'd like used when linking to you. (For example: "When linking to any portion of our teen site, please be sure to note that this site was developed by the XYZ public library.") And consider creating an advertising button ("click here to go to the XYZ Library's Teen Page") that could be offered for others to use as the link to your site. If you include the button on your site with information about how to add a link to your site, others can simply copy the image to use it on their sites.

UPKEEP

Creating your site takes a lot of work and effort, but once the site is up and running, the work has not ended. Instead of spending time deciding how to design your site and what colors to use, you now must keep up with making sure the links you have are still valid. In addition, if you've included any pages that have timely information, you must remember to keep it timely. There's nothing worse than accessing a "current events" calendar, only to see what was happening six months ago! In addition, you can now take time to expand the site. Create new Webographies and review the ones you already have up; see if there are new or better resources available.

On the other hand, repeat users will be frustrated if your site changes too often. Users come back to find resources that helped them in the past, and constant changes to the design and format of your site can be confusing. Add links when they contribute something important to what your site offers, and delete links when they no longer offer useful information.

Automated link checkers can be helpful in catching "bad URLs," but remember that they may interpret a page saying, "We've moved to a new address" as a "successful connection," so you also need to perform manual checks.

Consider offering an e-mail link for users to give "corrections and suggestions" for the site. You will receive many more accurate notices of connection errors and changes of address this way as well as receiving notice about some great sites, which may have gone unnoticed by you before.

Your timetable for working on the site, whether it's to fix existing errors or to expand the site, needs to be consistent and "doable" for your working situation. The following is a sample maintenance timetable, which you can adapt for your needs.

Daily—Updates to existing links on your site (such as address changes) should be made immediately. Incorrect addresses can point your users to places you would never want a patron (of any age) to explore!

Monthly—Make the time to physically check all of your links, making sure everything connects to the place (the site and section within the site) that it should. Examine assignment and program notices and remove anything that has passed its due date. Consider moving assignment notices to an archive, which can be useful both to the students who are making up work, and for you to use as a starting point when the assignment comes back next year.

Quarterly—Use this time to add substance to the site you have. Add new topics and booklists, or update the resources given on an existing list. Consider dropping little-used resources or subjects whose time has come and gone (this is particularly important if you include links to movie sites or links to celebrity home pages).

Annually—Review the overall appearance and usability of the site. Make sure that after all of your updates over the course of the year, the site is clean, is easy to navigate, and meets the needs of your community. Major changes to the appearance of your site should be reserved for this time. Consider doing this review at the end of the summer so you can promote the "new and revised" site in your back-to-school materials.

ON-LINE RESOURCES (FOR THE CREATION AND MAINTENANCE OF A SITE)

- **Bobby**, http://www.cast.org/bobby/. Visit Bobby after you've created your site, and have Bobby evaluate your site for accessibility concerns. Take the suggestions given and work to improve your site's accessibility. Once your site has passed Bobby's test, you can add one of their "Bobby Approved" graphics to your site.
- **Lynx Viewer**, http://www.delorie.com/web/lynxview.html. Try this site to get an idea of how your Web pages display in a text-only format. This site also offers a "Lynx Inspected" graphic for you to use.
- **PageResource**, http://www.pageresource.com/. PageResource has a collection of tutorials and style sheets for the beginner Web designer.
- **Virtual YA Index**, http://www.yahelp.suffolk.lib.ny.us/virtual.html. Use the Virtual YA Index to see how other libraries have developed their sites for teens. The sites range from basic to high tech, and all can help to show you what can be done with the Web.
- **Web Accessibility Initiative (WAI)**, http://www.w3.org/WAI/. WAI works in coordination with organizations around the world pursuing accessibility of the Web through five primary areas of work: technology, guidelines, tools, education and outreach, and research and development.
- **Web Pages That Suck**, http://www.webpagesthatsuck.com/. Use Web Pages That Suck to learn what to do by seeing real examples of what not to do. A tongue-in-cheek teaching method points out many of the common style errors found on Web pages and explains why some things that look very cool should just not be used (or be used only with discretion) in a user-friendly Web site.

ON-LINE RESOURCES TO CONSIDER USING
IN YOUR TEEN SITE

- **Go Ask Alice**, http://www.goaskalice.columbia.edu/. Go Ask Alice! is the controversial on-line health question and answer service produced by Alice!, Columbia University's Health Education Program, a division of Columbia University Health and Related Services. The mission of Go Ask Alice! is to increase access to, and use of, health information by providing factual, in-depth, straightforward, and nonjudgmental information to assist readers' decision-making about relationships; sexuality; sexual health; emotional health; fitness; nutrition; alcohol, nicotine, and other drugs; and general health. If your teens have the questions, "Alice!" gives the answers.

- **High School Hub**, http://www.highschoolhub.org/hub/hub. cfm. High School Hub provides access to free educational resources for high school students. It features on-line learning activities, an ongoing teen poetry contest, a reference collection, college information, and subject guides for English, mathematics, science, social studies, world languages, art, music, and health.

- **Occupational Outlook Handbook**, http://www.bls.gov/oco/. The standard resource for career information, the Occupational Outlook Handbook is great for teens who are thinking about and planning for their futures as well as teens who have been assigned to investigate a career path.

- **OutProud: The National Coalition for Gay, Lesbian, Bisexual, and Transgender Youth**, http://www.outproud.org/. OutProud serves the needs of gay, lesbian, and questioning youth by providing advocacy information, resources, and peer support. Their goal is to "help queer youth become happy, successful, confident, and vital gay, lesbian, and bisexual adults."

- **Reading Rants: Out of the Ordinary Teen Booklists**, http://tln. lib.mi.us/~amutch/jen/lists.html. Created by middle school librarian and voracious reader Jennifer Hubert Swan, Reading Rants is a cool collection of booklists for teens who are looking for something a little different to read. The topic-driven lists include young adult and adult titles, new and classic books, as well as award-winning authors and titles. With lists such as "Bare Bones: Honest Fiction about Weight and Eating Disorders" and

"Stoned: Druggie Fiction for the Teenaged Masses," it's easy to see why teens and young adult librarians enjoy Jennifer Hubert Swan's picks.

• **Spank! Youth Culture Online**, http://www.spankmag.com/. Focusing on youth issues, interests, and life in general, Spank! is self-described as the first youth lifestyle magazine in cyberspace. It is published on a continual basis for readers throughout North America, although they have visitors from around the world. Spank's discussion forum format contains coverage of entertainment, music, life, recreation, fashion, education, employment, and pop culture. Their editorial board is comprised of volunteers, ranging in age from 14 to 28, and publishing professionals to ensure the magazine remains focused on youth interests. Spank's publishing policies hold to the Canadian Charter of Rights and Freedoms, and will remove posts that conflict with the spirit of that document (comments based on racism, sexism, or other forms of discrimination).

CONCLUSION

Creating and developing an on-line collection is an opportunity to expand your library services to teens. There are many different ways for libraries to build their Web presence, and though you might not have your hand in the actual development (or maintenance) of the teen site, these are some of the important aspects of an on-line collection for teens that you should be aware of. Through the careful selection of links, the inclusion of useful content, and an appealing design, your on-line teen collection may become a favorite of your teen community.

7

TEENS GOT (WAY MORE THAN) GAME: INTERACTIVE SOFTWARE AND GAMES

Valerie A. Ott

Given the technologically savvy nature of teens, developing a CD-ROM and game collection for your library is a great idea. Quite frankly, many teens do not enjoy reading, and view the library only as a place filled with books. As a result, they would never dream of coming to the library for recreational games, or to check out CDs that could help with their homework. Adding CD-ROMs and games to your teen collection will surprise and delight those teens who think the library has nothing for them.

This chapter will examine "other" types of materials that appeal to teens, but aren't commonplace in library collections—educational CD-ROMs and games. Information related to these media includes:

- Definitions of each type
- Advantages, challenges, and considerations of each
- How to prepare for building these collections
- How to select items for your collection, as well as how to maintain it
- The various types of game playing systems, as well as personal computer platforms
- Marketing and merchandising the collection

Although many of the following terms are used interchangeably, they will be used according to these specific definitions throughout this chapter.

- **CD-ROM**—stands for Compact Disc-Read Only Memory. Reference CD-ROMs are educational and searchable in nature and are often loaded onto a library's server for in-house use due to their higher price tags (e.g., *Masterplots Complete* by Salem Press retails for $750). Less expensive, single-content CD-ROMs are often loaned out to patrons to be used at home (e.g., *Essential Clipart* by Summitsoft retails for $14.99).
- **Computer Game**—any game that is in CD format and can be played on a PC or Macintosh computer using a keyboard as an input device. These can be educational or recreational, but this chapter will concentrate on the recreational variety.
- **Video Game**—any game contained on a cartridge that must be inserted into a games console to be viewed on a television. Input devices for video games depend on the game and the console, but usually consist of a handheld controller, such as a joystick. Virtually all of these games are recreational in nature.

ADVANTAGES, CHALLENGES, AND CONSIDERATIONS FOR THESE ITEMS

Adding different formats to your teen collection, while progressive and exciting, can also create new challenges. Here are some points to consider before creating the collection.

Advantages to adding these to your collections:

- Attract new teens to your library
- Provide materials teens/families may not be able to purchase
- Teens attracted to technology will think of the library as a "cooler" place
- Teens are great resources for information in these areas—get them involved

---

Advantage: Adding different formats could attract a new clientele to your library. Those who may never have set foot in your library before may now be attracted to something you have to offer.

Challenge: CD-ROMs, computer games, and video games may serve only a small population—i.e., those who own computers and/or game consoles.

Consideration: Consider assessing your community before spending a lot of money on these formats. Through surveying your users, you may be able to estimate what portion of your population owns and/or can afford home computers and game consoles, to see if the money spent would be proportional to the percent of the population served.

Advantage: While many families may be able to afford a home computer or a game console, the software can add up. By loaning CD-ROMs and games to your teen patrons to take home and try for free, you may be providing materials some cannot afford.

Challenge: Video games in particular can be expensive. Currently, most are about $50 apiece, making it difficult to both develop a large collection, and keep it current. These items may also be at high risk for theft.

Consideration: Be aware of the newest, hottest games on the market by reading consumer reviews, then make your selections prudently. If a game has had several spin-offs and you're not sure which to purchase, you may consider spending a little more and buying the "deluxe" version to get more bang for your buck. Poll your teens to see which game console is most popular, and buy video games solely for that format; this way you won't spread your budget thin by trying to buy several games for each type of console. If your library uses a security system, make sure these items get "tagged." Also, consider shelving these items in a high-traffic and easily monitored area.

Advantage: Plain and simple, teens are attracted to technology. Even those who don't own a computer or game console will view the library as a "cooler" place to be if their peers start taking advantage of your new collection.

Challenge: The kind of teen who is attracted to the library *solely* for its technology and recreational game collection may not be interested in educational resources you have to offer. This may spawn criticism from more traditional users of the library.

Consideration: Use your new computer and video game collection as the hook that draws teens in, but try eye-catching and strategically placed displays to promote your educational CD-ROMs as well. A sixteen-year-old boy may come to the library only in search of the newest game, but with the right promotion, he may also leave with a CD-ROM that will help him with his science fair project. Keep in mind, however, that providing recreational materials is an important function of any library in and of itself.

Advantage: There is great teen-demand for more technology in libraries; if and when you decide to add CD-ROMs and games to your collection, there probably won't be a shortage of teen suggestions as to which title you should buy next.

Challenge: As many teen librarians will tell you, there is often a difference between popularity and quality; it may seem difficult to evaluate electronic sources.

Consideration: The same standards for evaluating books should apply to reference CD-ROMs. Accuracy of information, authority, a thoroughly cross-referenced index, intuitive layout and design, age-appropriateness, and other standards of evaluation easily translate to electronic sources. While there are special considerations to keep in mind such as compatibility, don't reinvent the wheel when evaluating electronic sources. Read reviews, familiarize yourself with the publishers, and try them yourself, just as you would when selecting books. In terms of computer and video games, rely heavily on your teen patrons for suggestions, but read as many reviews as you can about each title before making purchases. You will find a list of reviewing sources later in this chapter.

PRELIMINARY WORK

Doing some homework is the next step you should take after considering what the implications are for your library when developing a CD-ROM and game collection. In other words, consider the formats available, what publishing companies have to offer, the range of titles available for your chosen format, and the cost.

Reference CD-ROMs

Some may consider adding reference CD-ROMs to the library's collection to be superfluous because a large amount of information can already be accessed through the Internet. However, searching the Internet is often frustrating and time-consuming for students due to the vast amounts of information available and the questionable accuracy of the content contained on Web sites with dubious authority. Reference CD-ROMs, on the other hand, still provide tech-savvy teens with the joy of electronic access, but are content-specific, authoritative, and often rich in graphics, making research less of a hassle and more exciting. Viewed in this light, reference CD-ROMs are a wonderful supplement to the Internet access your library already provides.

Disclaimer

Because the technologies in this area change frequently, please keep in mind that your teens may well know more about the games and technologies that are "cutting edge." Be prepared to seek their advice on a regular basis.

When choosing reference CD-ROMs to make available to your teen patrons through in-house use, familiarize yourself with the type of computers your library owns and the operating systems they use. Generally, most CD-ROM titles are available for both IBM and Macintosh computers. Make sure that the software you want to purchase is compatible with your library's operating system (OS). While most libraries these days use Microsoft Windows as their OS, you must also pay attention to the version your library uses. The following list contains the most common versions of Windows used in libraries, some of which are outdated and indicated as such with an asterisk:

- 9.x Systems
  - Windows 95*
  - Windows 98*
  - Windows Me*

- NT (New Technology) Systems
  - Windows NT 4.0*
  - Windows 2000 Professional
  - Windows XP or XP Pro

Some libraries do, however, use Macintosh computers. In this case, the most common operating systems available are:

- Mac OS 8.5*
- Mac OS 9
- Mac OS X

If your library does, in fact, use an older system, you should know that you may be limited in terms of the range of software titles available on the market that are compatible with that OS.

Likewise, when purchasing less expensive educational CD-ROMs for your circulating collection, it is still important to pay attention to compatibility issues. In this case, though, you may want to collect CD-ROMs for both IBM and Macintosh operating systems, since it would be hard to guess what OS each teen uses at home. In terms of the version of the OS, again, you will be limited to the product(s) currently on the market.

This brings up the issue of currency. Since Microsoft, for instance, seems to produce a new version of Windows on a frequent basis, it would seem that the CD-ROMs you purchase one year may not be compatible with your teens' home computers the following year. A good rule of thumb to keep in mind is that operating systems usually have a life span of three years. For example, since Microsoft XP was produced in 2002, it will probably be a viable OS until at least 2005. It is safe to say, therefore, that any software you purchase for your circulating collection today will be good for three years, at which point you will probably find that many of the discs have been damaged, been lost, or fallen off in circulation because of decreased popularity or outdated information. To put it another way, it is important to stay current with technological changes and trends, but by the time three years have passed, you will likely be ready to purchase new CD-ROMs for your collection anyway.

There are literally thousands of companies that publish educational software for computers. The PEP (Parents, Educators, and Publishers) Registry of Educational Software Publishers (http://www.microweb.

com/pepsite/Software/publishers.html) lists over 2,200 such manufac-
turers, with direct links to their Web sites. Here is a small sampling of
some of the more common companies with which you may be familiar,
along with the subjects in which they specialize:

- ABC-CLIO—history, government, and war
- Cambridge Educational—wide range of subjects covered
- Corel—desktop publishing
- Dorling-Kindersley—graphically rich encyclopedias on a variety of topics
- Encyclopaedia Britannica Educational Corporation—authoritative encyclopedias
- Kaplan Interactive—mathematics education and standardized tests
- Rand McNally—geography

The range of available CD-ROM titles is broad, but collection development of this format becomes easier when the titles are grouped into
these main categories of particular use or interest to teens:

- Almanacs
- Fine Art and Music
- Business and Industry
- Desktop Publishing
- Dictionaries
- Education and Career
- Encyclopedias
- Health and Medicine
- History
- Language
- Literature
- Maps and Atlases
- Science and Nature
- Religion
- Social Issues

Prices for educational CD-ROMs vary greatly. As previously noted, reference software such as encyclopedias can be quite expensive, with many costing as much as $200 or more. Many reference CD-ROMs will be one-time purchases for your library. But some, like almanacs, have information that changes yearly. These are generally viewed as subscription CD-ROMs, with updates available for purchase every year. If you have your eye on the bottom line, you may want to stay with the print or on-line version of such sources and opt for reference CD-ROMs only when their usefulness is not dependent on how current they are, such as those for language or literature. On the other hand, single-topic programs, such as *Resume Maker Deluxe 9.0* by Individual Software, are much more affordable, most costing $20 to $50 each. These smaller price tags make it easy to develop a good core collection of circulating CD-ROMs. The choices you make, therefore, will not be unlike those you make when developing a book collection in that the most expensive items you purchase will probably be used as reference material, while the less pricey programs can be circulated freely.

Computer Games and Video Games

According to the Entertainment Software Association, or ESA (http://www.theesa.com/pressroom.html), 60 percent of all Americans play computer and/or video games. Of the most frequent players of computer games, 34 percent are under 18 years old. And of the most frequent players of video games, 46 percent are under 18 years old. Clearly, the fact that teens comprise a very large percentage of the electronic gaming population is hard to ignore. Furthermore, while it may be obvious to you that adding computer and/or video games to your library's collection will attract teenaged boys, don't think these formats don't interest girls. The ESA states that 43 percent of those who play computer and/or video games are female.

Chances are your budget constraints won't allow you to purchase each title in computer game format *and* video game format. Therefore, it is important to know the difference between the two types of gaming software.

First, recognize that while PCs can vary from library to library and home to home in terms of operating system, memory, graphics, and sound capabilities, all machines of a particular model of games console are identical to one another. In other words, any PlayStation 2 video game will be compatible with any PlayStation 2 games console without any variations in quality from unit to unit.

While this is the biggest difference between PCs and games consoles, there are also differences in format and prices. The choices you make in terms of format and operating system for computer games are much the same as when developing an educational software collection. Since you will probably be circulating your computer game collection, rather than loading each one onto your library's server, it would be wise to purchase computer games for both PCs and Macintosh computers. As was the case with reference and other educational CD-ROMs, the current market will determine what version of operating system the computer games will need to operate properly.

Computer games range in price from $9.99 to over $50, depending on such things as the level of interactivity, the number of players who can participate simultaneously, and the sophistication of the graphics. For example, *Vegas Games 2000* by 3DO sells for $19.99, can entertain only one player at a time, and has limited input options, making its level of interactivity quite low. In contrast, *Star Wars Galaxies: An Empire Divided* by LucasArts Entertainment is $49.99 and is considered a massively multiplayer on-line role-playing game (MMORPG), allowing for thousands of interaction possibilities among the characters. It would be wise to collect computer games of varying prices since there is a direct correlation between the price and sophistication of each game.

Switching gears to video games, it is essential to know the features and capabilities of each brand of game console before making selection decisions about which format of game cartridges to buy. There are two main types of consoles: home machines and handheld devices. The three home machines on the market today are the Microsoft Xbox ($200), the Nintendo GameCube ($150), and the Sony PlayStation 2 ($200). The only handheld device popular right now is the Nintendo Game Boy Advance ($70).

There are slight variations among the three home machines available now. The Xbox and the PlayStation 2 are the most similar, but the Xbox has the advantage of a hard disk drive for saving downloaded games, and a port to connect directly to the Internet. On the other hand, the PlayStation 2 can play DVDs right out of the box, while the Xbox requires a $30 kit to play them. Right now, the big advantage the PlayStation 2 has over the Xbox is the range of games available. Owners of the PlayStation 2 can play games made for the older version of the console as well, while the Xbox is so new to the market that the amount of games available is limited.

Nintendo's GameCube is $50 cheaper than the other two home machines, but it does not have the capability to connect to the Internet or play DVDs, with or without a DVD kit. It is important to note that the games produced for this machine are traditionally geared more to children and teens; however, the GameCube currently has the smallest library of titles in comparison to all the other machines.

The Nintendo Game Boy Advance is the most affordable, and the most portable, machine on the market. For these reasons alone, this device is popular with teens, despite its need for batteries, and complaints that the screen is hard to see in certain lighting. Obviously, this little machine cannot play DVDs or connect to the Internet, but Nintendo is scheduled to release a device that will allow the Game Boy to be plugged into the GameCube. There are many games to choose from for this format; next to the PlayStation 2, the Game Boy Advance has the largest library of games.

Like computer games, video games also cost about $50 or less. Specifically, games for home consoles (Xbox, GameCube, and PlayStation 2) are $49.99, while cartridges for the only handheld device (Game Boy Advance) are $29.99 and $39.99.

Once you have grasped the differences between computer games and video games, it is simple to outline their similarities in terms of publishers, range of titles, and ratings. First, there are over 100 companies that produce recreational software for PCs and game consoles, and many of them publish titles as both computer games *and* video games. For example, Electronic Arts publishes *The Sims* for Windows and Macintosh operating systems as well as for PlayStation 2. Some other companies with which you may be familiar are listed below:

- Acclaim, http://www.acclaim.com
- Atari, http://www.atari.com
- Capcom, http://www.capcom.com
- MacPlay, http://macplay.com
- Maxis, http://www.maxis.com
- Microsoft, http://microsoft.com/games
- Sega, http://www.sega.com
- Sony, http://www.sony.com

Four Fat Chicks (http://fourfatchicks.com/Rants/Misc/Companies. shtml) have compiled an extensive list of game software publishers on their Web site that may help familiarize you with this segment of the publishing industry.

With regard to the range of recreational titles available for both PCs and game consoles, it is convenient to break them down into the following basic categories.

- Action/Adventure (e.g., *Tomb Raider* by Eidos)
- Sports (e.g., *Backyard Baseball* by Infogames Entertainment)
- Racing/Driving (e.g. *Burnout* by Acclaim)
- Fighting (e.g., *Tekken* by Namco)
- Puzzle/Strategy (e.g., *Tetris* by THQ)
- Role-Playing (e.g., *The Sims* by Electronic Arts)
- Shooter (e.g., *Doom* by Activision)

According to the ESA, strategy games and role-playing games were the best-selling genres in 2001.

Most games produced for computers and game consoles are rated by the Entertainment Software Review Board (ESRB). The ratings are as follows:

- EC—Early Childhood
- KA—Kids to Adults
- E—Everyone
- T—Teen
- M—Mature
- A—Adults Only

Intellectual Freedom Issues

Many of the games marketed toward teens are violent in nature and possess either an "M" or an "A." Also, the "T"-rated items possess a degree of violence or other content that might possibly be problematic. Have plans in place for the handling of challenges you might face when collecting these items. For example, parents might lodge a complaint because their 10-year-old checks out a "T"-rated item. It may be more difficult to argue basic intellectual freedom issues for a game as opposed to other library materials. Be prepared.

The ESA reports that since the ESRB began rating games in 1994, 62 percent of the games produced have been rated E for Everyone and 25 percent have been rated T for Teen, making this format chock-full of games that are age-appropriate for your teenaged patrons.

PREVIEW, REVIEW, AND REVISE

As previously stated, the same basic evaluation standards for print sources should apply to reference and other educational software as well. Authority, accuracy, grade level, tone, scope, cost, and currency are all criteria just as important to remember when selecting reference CD-ROMs as when selecting books. There are a couple of special considerations to bear in mind, however, in addition to the compatibility issues that have already been described.

First, instead of making certain that there is an adequately cross-referenced index, ensure that users can navigate the source with ease. Similar to navigating a Web site, teens should be able to find the menu and search the source for topics without much effort. Reviewers often use the word "intuitive" to describe how the navigational process should occur; if a CD-ROM is described as such, rest assured that your teen patrons will not have to struggle to find what they're looking for.

Secondly, unlike books, CD-ROMs often have audio features and animated graphics. Since these features are often what attracts teens to electronic sources in the first place, make sure that the sound and visual features are of high quality and are not too cheesy.

Usually, nothing can take the place of previewing sources prior to selection. But in the case of game software especially, this is not always feasible, for two reasons. First, if you are not a computer/video game aficionado, you probably aren't the best person to evaluate such formats. Secondly, it is unlikely that your library will have a PlayStation 2, Xbox, GameCube, or Game Boy with which to preview the cartridges. Reliable review sources are a staple for selecting any source, especially for electronic sources with which you may not be familiar. The following list contains a list of tried and true review sources that will help make your life easier when selecting educational CD-ROMs, computer games, and video games.

- **Amazon**, http://www.amazon.com. You've probably used Amazon to find product information and reviews for books, but don't forget that there are "Software" and "Computer and Video Games" sections, too. With its familiar five-star ratings and consumer reviews, this is a great review source with which to start.

- **Children's Software Revue**, http://www.childrenssoftware. com/. This bimonthly journal contains helpful articles and software reviews for middle and high school students. Educational CD-ROMs, computer games, and all formats of video games are covered here on a five-star rating system with All-Star Awards given to the products most highly recommended by reviewers and student testers, making it easy to pick out high-quality titles. An alphabetical directory of new releases is contained in each issue. Visitors to the Web site must have a password provided with a subscription to the journal in order to access reviews.

- **Four Fat Chicks**, http://fourfatchicks.com/review_index.shtml. This Web site is more irreverent than some review journals, but it has loads of thoroughly written reviews for computer games and video games. Each review contains a section called "The Lowdown" in which system requirements, price, availability, screenshots, and player feedback are provided. There is also a "Verdict" bestowed on each game with tongue-in-cheek graphics representing the reviewer's feelings about the title. While this site gives you more information than you probably need about the strategy, gimmicks, and graphics of each game, it is best to keep in mind that it wasn't created as a selection tool for librarians. In other words, little attention is given to the age-appropriateness or teen appeal of each game.

- **MacGamer**, http://www.macledge.com/features/index.php?cat =1&go.x=10&go.y=4. This site contains seven years' worth of Macintosh computer game reviews. Similar to Four Fat Chicks, this site wasn't intended as a selection tool for librarians, but it does thoroughly break down the positive and negative aspects of each game. The titles are rated on a scale of one to five with a concise list of their pros and cons at the end of each review. Again, ESRB ratings are not included to help determine age-appropriateness, so use this site as a supplement to other review sources.

- **School Library Journal**, http://www.slj.com. This monthly journal is another source with which you're probably already familiar. In its Multimedia Review section, there are a few educational

CD-ROMs reviewed each month. This review journal has the reputation of upholding uncompromising standards for its readers. Reviews on the Web site can only be accessed with a paid subscription.

- **SuperKids Educational Software Review**, http://www.super kids.com/. Each review on this site gives a one to five rating to a CD-ROM or learning game for its educational value, kid appeal, and ease of use as well as a "bottom line" section that succinctly explains who should buy the title and why. System requirements and age levels are also given for each title. In addition to a huge, searchable database of reviews, this site contains a best seller list, educational tools and games, product support, and featured articles. Best of all, all of the information can be accessed for free!

- **techLEARNING**, http://www.techlearning.com/content/resources /product_guide/. This site has over 300 reviews of educational CD-ROMs that can be searched by subject, platform, and grade level. The reviews aren't lengthy, but do give basic information about each title, such as price, publisher, subjects covered, and grade level. This site is a good backup source to these other review sources, but don't expect to find a comprehensive listing of titles here.

Marketing and Merchandising

Once you have decided which materials to purchase for your new electronic collection, it is important to promote them so your teen patrons become aware of the new items you have to offer. In terms of marketing, first make sure to mention your new collection in any newsletters your library may publish, on your library's Web site, and in any correspondence with your teen advisory board. You may consider giving the collection a catchy name, or designing a logo that will lend visual consistency to your promotions. Obviously, you will aim most of your marketing tactics to your teen patrons; however, don't forget teachers. Sending a list of your newly acquired educational titles to area schools may be a good idea.

Displays

Creating eye-catching displays is an effective method for merchandising your electronic collection within the library. Your computer and video games will probably fly off the shelves without any promotion, but educational resources may need a bit of pushing.

- Dedicate a spot on your teen Web site to featuring a "CD-ROM of the Month." Advertise the perks of using that resource, and provide a link to it so teens can try it out for themselves.
- Fill an acrylic cube with subject-related realia to promote your resources. For example, during science fair season, fill the cube with beakers and test tubes and put it beside the computer loaded with *Science Smart* by Mindscape. Or, towards graduation time, fill the cube with fake money, a checkbook, and a graduation cap to advertise *Resume Maker Deluxe* by Individual Software or *Quicken* by Intuit.
- Post signs near the library's print encyclopedias advertising your *World Book* CD-ROM, or ask the reference staff to wear "Ask Me About . . ." buttons to promote, for example, the use of *Masterplots Complete* for book reports and critical analysis papers.
- Take pictures of teens using your in-house CD-ROM collection and display them on a poster or bulletin board loaded with information about your new collection. You may also be able to post these posters in your local schools with permission from the school library media specialists or principals.

Programming

Programming is a more applied approach to promoting your newly added formats, and is ideal for CD-ROMs and games, since they have qualities that are hard to describe without hands-on experience.

- Class visits—Invite area teachers to bring their classes to the library for a field trip. Give a brief description of each new CD-ROM, then let the students try them out in small groups. Serve small snacks as "bytes to eat" for a mid-session refreshment, and pass out a brochure that explains how each resource can help with future homework assignments.
- Sneak Peaks—Pick the newest, hottest games you have and invite teens to bring their Game Boys so they can be the first to try them out. Have participants write short reviews on each game, which can then be included in a "Tech Tips" section of your teen news-

letter. Lastly, be sure to get written permission from teen authors or their parents to print their reviews if your library policy calls for this.

- Video Game Tournament—Let teens compete against each other on the game of their choice for prizes or just bragging rights. For added effect, project the game on a movie screen or simply a white wall; every participant can view the action this way.

- Swap Meet—Have teens bring in their own game cartridges to swap with others. This program could reveal what the most coveted game of the moment is, which will, in turn, help you add popular titles to your collection.

On-line Resources for CD-ROM Collection Development

- **Curriculum Lab CD-ROM Collection**, http://www.library. vanderbilt.edu/peabody/books/currlabcds/. The curriculum lab at the Peabody Library of Vanderbilt University has a core collection of educational CD-ROMs for K-12 students. This site is organized by subject, and lists each CD-ROM alphabetically with a brief annotation.

- **Educational Software Companies on the Internet**, http://www. geocities.com/Athens/8259/softman.html. This list is made with homeschoolers in mind; the companies are listed alphabetically with brief annotations.

- **EPICENTER**, http://www.epicent.com/software/header.html. EPICENTER stands for Education Process Improvement Center, which is an education consulting company. This list of educational software products is searchable by product name, publishing company, and subject. Each product is briefly described and is assigned an appropriate grade level.

- **Mid-South Educational Software Clearinghouse (MSESC)**, http://www.people.memphis.edu/~jsiegel/msesc.htm. The University of Memphis established the MSESC in order to collect software programs from all over the world that address the special needs of students. The link to the specific software housed at the MSESC isn't particularly helpful by itself, but the link to their reviews of the products is a great selection tool. There is also a listing of software sites that offer free shareware and demos.

- **PEP Registry of Educational Software Publishers**, http://microweb.com/pepsite/Software/publishers.html. PEP stands for "Parents, Educators, and Publishers" who want to promote students' use of technology. Their alphabetical list of links to software publishers is the most comprehensive on the Internet.

On-line Resources for Computer/Video Game Collection Development

- **Entertainment Software Rating Board (ESRB)**, http://www.esrb.org. The ESRB site is designed as a guide to understanding the game rating system. Visitors to this site can enter the name of a game to find out its rating, browse a list of participating publishers, and link to other organizations that promote the ESRB rating system.

- **Entertainment Software Association (ESA)**, http://www.idsa.com. The ESA is an organization dedicated to supporting the public relations needs of recreational software companies. This site is helpful to librarians primarily for its statistics about the electronic gaming industry and its customers.

- **Four Fat Chicks**, http://fourfatchicks.com/index.shtml. This site reviews computer, video, and on-line games. In addition to writing thorough reviews, the authors of this site also do some minor troubleshooting for your hardware, give updates on upcoming releases and, of particular interest to your teen patrons, they also give "walkthroughs" of many games.

- **MacGamer**, http://www.macledge.com. This is a huge review site specifically for games designed for Macintosh computers. There are also weekly columns and news stories as well as a download center.

- **Microsoft Xbox Video Game System**, http://www.microsoft.com/catalog/display.asp?site=10463&subid=22&pg=1. Describes the features and system requirements of the Xbox, but more importantly, the site lists Xbox games as well as those games compatible with PCs. In addition, there are links to Microsoft gaming sites and resources.

- **Nintendo Game Systems**, http://www.nintendo.com/systems/ index.jsp. Similar site to the Microsoft Xbox site, but for Nintendo products.

- **PlayStation.com**, http://www.us.playstation.com/. Similar site to both the Xbox and the Nintendo sites, but for Sony products. This site, however, also includes a helpful list of the top 10 best-selling PlayStation 2 games.

- **Video Game Answer Man**, http://vgaman.tripod.com/. This site has a wealth of information about each video game system. Although it is not as sophisticatedly designed as some of the above resources, Video Game Answer Man gives honest advice about each system, which will lend some insight as to which format of game cartridge you should collect for your library.

CONCLUSION

Adding CD-ROMs, computer games, and video games to your teen collection is great PR for your library because it acknowledges the interests and tech-savvy nature of your young adult patrons. Discriminating teens will be pleasantly surprised by the presence of these new formats in the library, which may lay the foundation for future library use for either educational or recreational purposes. Once you've become familiar with these electronic sources, it will be a pleasure to collect, promote, and circulate them as wonderful supplements to the Internet access and print collections you already provide.

8

SHELVING AND DISPLAY OPTIONS

C. Allen Nichols

Librarians with shelves full of library materials can no longer sit idly by and expect teens (or any customers for that matter) to rush into their libraries and check out materials.

Times have changed, and so have the demands on a teenager's life. Teens' schedules are filled with homework, extracurricular activities, home responsibilities, work, and more. Because the Internet is quick and available 24/7, teens now turn to the Internet for information and entertainment. If you don't believe me, watch the teens in your library after school one day to learn where their first stop is. My guess . . . an Internet computer terminal, that is, if one is not already in use when they enter the building. So, while the teens are in your building using the computer, or just hanging out with friends, what types of things can you do to make teens stand up and notice that you have materials in all formats purchased with them in mind?

One thing you can do is to make sure your collection is displayed/shelved in an appealing way that invites teens to pick up and examine the materials you have for them. If your shelving and displaying efforts consist of spines on a shelf, I do not believe teens will even turn in that direction once their time on the computer ends. The reason is simple; historically, surveys have shown that teens do not automatically turn to librarians for assistance in locating items. Teens prefer browsing and searching on their own.

I believe an important factor for any collection within the young adult area is the proper shelving and displaying of the items in it. On the pages that follow are some shelving and display furnishings that will assist your marketing and merchandising efforts. While similar items are available from any number of library suppliers, the pictures that follow are reprinted through the generous permission of DEMCO. These appear in the company's 2003 Annual Catalog, as well as on their Web site at http://www.demco.com.

The advantage of many of the products highlighted here is that they allow for the face-front display of the items placed in or on them. Since the alternative formats discussed in this book are often identified with teen popular culture, the face-front display of these items is more appealing to teen browsers and will "grab their attention" better than any other shelving arrangement.

Figure 8.1
Compact Magazine Spinner

This Compact Magazine Spinner is separated into sixteen pockets that hold thirteen magazines or comic books each. (This has room for back-issues.) The Spinner holds over 200 magazines or comics in all.

Figure 8.2
Durham Con-Tur Steel Literature Rack

The Durham Con-Tur Steel Literature Rack is composed of five individual racks that can be added together for expansion. Each of these racks holds 23 titles. The titles are visible and the curved pockets are designed to keep the magazines and comics standing upright, as opposed to falling forward.

Figure 8.3
Compact Magazine Display

This Compact Magazine Display tucks neatly onto the end of your shelving ranges and eliminates the dead space. Each of the eight pockets displays its contents in face-front manner, and can hold 19 magazines or comic books.

Figure 8.4
Mar-Line Periodical Display and Storage System

This unit, the Mar-Line Periodical Display and Storage System, is a compartmentalized display unit. It allows the current issue of each magazine to be presented face-front on a flip-up lid, while containing the back issues in a compartment behind the lid. This particular unit is available in a variety of 6, 9, 15, or 20 compartments.

Figure 8.5
See-All Storage Shelf

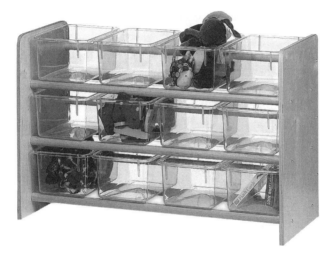

Sometimes the best way to display comic books is in a bin that can be easily accessed and sorted through by the teens. The See-All Storage Shelf has 12 clear trays to allow for easy viewing, while keeping different titles separated.

Figure 8.6
DEMCO Multimedia Browsing Bins

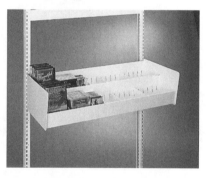

For those with limited floor space for shelving and displaying audiovisual items, consider replacing a couple of bookshelves with DEMCO Multimedia Browsing Bins. These fit into library shelving, are available in one- and two-tier options, and hold a variety of different audiovisual items.

Figure 8.7
"A" Frame Multimedia Shelving

Another unit that holds and displays a variety of audiovisual materials is the "A" Frame Multimedia Shelving unit. Constructed of steel grid, it has 12 total shelves (6 on each side) and holds videos, DVDs, or audiobooks.

Figure 8.8
DEMCO Face-out Multimedia Display

The DEMCO Face-out Multimedia Display holds 84 multimedia items, from videos to DVDs to audiobooks, not to mention compact discs. All of the items on the unit are visible thanks to the face-front arrangement of the unit.

Figure 8.9
Multimedia A-frame Display

The Multimedia A-frame Display has shelves that contain a zigzag fixture to create an eye-appealing face-front display. Again, this unit holds videos, audiobooks, DVDs, and CDs.

Figure 8.10
Mobile Media Cart

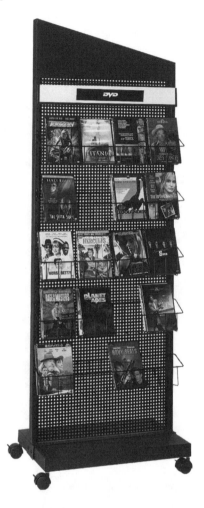

For those displays on-the-go, the Mobile Media Cart allows for variety in the location of your displays. It also is a great way to share a display unit with other departments because it is not fixed in any one location. For budgetary purposes, the costs can be shared by different departments to minimize the effect on tight library budgets. This is a double-sided unit that offers a number of accessories and types of shelves to hold an assortment of audiovisual items.

Figure 8.11
Randal Curved Multimedia Display

The Randal Curved Multimedia Display is an eye-appealing way to display any number of audiovisual items. The shelves come with adjustable dividers to fit varying widths of items.

Figure 8.12
Birch CD Display

For the smaller music collection or to highlight a particular musical genre, think about the Birch CD Display. This spinner includes three cubes that rotate individually, and it holds up to 300 CDs.

Figure 8.13
DEMCO "The Max" CD/DVD Floor Display

The DEMCO "The Max" CD/DVD Floor Display holds 640 CDs or 480 DVDs.

Figure 8.14
Videocassette Browser Bins

These Videocassette Browser Bins are for the smaller video collection, and can be placed on any table or countertop. The unit comes with adjustable dividers that will also allow it to hold CDs.

BIBLIOGRAPHY

Crawford, Walt. " 'Watch This, It's Good For You': Thoughts on Video and Libraries." In *Video Collection Development in Multi-Type Libraries: A Handbook*, 2nd ed., edited by Gary Handman. Westport, CT: Greenwood Press, 2002.

Dagg, Emily. "Graphic Novels in Children's and Young Adult Library Collections." Master's thesis, University of Washington, 1997.

Diamond Bookshelf (Catalog), Diamond Comic Distributors, 2002.

Eisner, Will. *Comics & Sequential Art*. Tamarac, FL: Poorhouse Press, 1985.

Franco, Debra. "A Primer on the Home Video Market." In *Video Collection Development in Multi-Type Libraries: A Handbook*, 2nd ed., edited by Gary Handman. Westport, CT: Greenwood Press, 2002.

Harker, Jean Gray. "Youth's Librarians Can Defeat Comics." *Library Journal* (December 1, 1948): 1705–1707, 1720.

Hegenberger, John. *Collector's Guide to Comic Books*. Radnor, PA: Wallace-Homestead Book Co., 1990.

LaMoore, Jeanne. "Graphic Novels for Middle School Readers: An Annotated Bibliography." Alternate plan paper, Mankato State University, 1998.

McCloud, Scott. *Reinventing Comics*. New York: HarperCollins, 2000.

———. *Understanding Comics*. New York: HarperCollins, 1994.

Nyberg, Amy Kiste. *Seal of Approval: The History of the Comics Code*. Jackson: University Press of Mississippi, 1998.

Owens, Thomas S. *Collecting Comic Books: A Young Person's Guide*. Brookfield, CT: Milbrook Press, 1995.

Rothschild, D. Aviva. *Graphic Novels: A Bibliographic Guide to Book-Length Comics*. Englewood, CO: Libraries Unlimited, 1995.

Schodt, Frederik L. *Manga! Manga! The World of Japanese Comics*. Tokyo, Japan: Kodansha International LTD, 1983, 1997.

Scott, Randall W. *Comics Librarianship: A Handbook*. Jefferson, NC: McFarland, 1990.

SJK [pseud.]. "Libraries to Arms!" *Wilson Library Bulletin*, 15 (1941): 670–671.

———. "The Comic Menace." *Wilson Library Bulletin*, 15 (1941): 846–847.

Trelease, Jim. *The New Read-Aloud Handbook*. New York: Penguin Books, 1989.

Vollman-Grone, Michael. "Public Library Video Collections." In *Video Collection Development in Multi-Type Libraries: A Handbook*, 2nd ed., edited by Gary Handman. Westport, CT: Greenwood Press, 2002.

Weiner, Stephen. *100 Graphic Novels for Public Libraries*. Northampton, MA: Kitchen Sink, 1996.

———. *The 101 Best Graphic Novels*. New York: NBM, 2001.

———. *The 101 Best Graphic Novels Supplement For Libraries: Starting & Maintaining a Graphic Novel Collection*. New York: NBM, 2001.

Williams, Gweneira and Jane Wilson. "They Like It Rough: In Defence of Comics." *Library Journal* (March 1, 1942): 204–206.

Wright, Ethel C. "A Public Library Experiments with the Comics." *Library Journal* (October 15, 1943): 832–835.

Zimmerman, Thomas. "What to Do about Comics." *Library Journal* (September 15, 1954): 1605–1607.

INDEX

ABOUT THE EDITOR AND CONTRIBUTORS

C. ALLEN NICHOLS is Director of the Wadsworth Public Library. Prior to this appointment, he served as teen librarian for most of his 23-year career in libraries. He holds an MLS degree from Kent State University and is currently working toward an MBA from Mississippi State University. A past president of the Ohio Library Association, Allen is also an active member of the Young Adult Library Services Association, currently serving as its fiscal officer. He has co-authored two books and, along with his wife Mary Anne, is series co-editor of the "Professional Guides for Young Adult Librarians" published by Libraries Unlimited.

CHRISTINE BORNE is the Teen Librarian at the Shaker Heights (Ohio) Public Library, and earned her M.L.I.S. from Kent State University in 2002. She is a member of ALA, YALSA, Ohio Library Council, and the Progressive Librarians Guild. She is also the list owner of NEXGENLIB-L, an internationally recognized listserv for librarians under age 30.

KEVIN FERST is presently Teen Librarian at the Regency Square Branch of the Jacksonville Public Library in Jacksonville, Florida. He is a member of ALA and YALSA. He graduated from the Kent State University School of Library and Information Science in December 2002. He also graduated from Kent State University with a B.A. in Philosophy in 1998. He has worked in a variety of settings, including a natural foods store, a homeless shelter, and an upholstery shop. His main interests include natural health and healing, art, simple living, and personal evolution.

TRACEY A. FIRESTONE is the Young Adult Specialist for the Suffolk Cooperative Library System, in Bellport, New York. She is also the Webmaster for the Young Adult Librarians' Home Page, the Virtual YA Index: Public Libraries with Young Adult Web Pages, and the New York Library Association's Youth Services Section, and is the chair of YALSA's Teen Web Advisory Committee.

SARAH FLOWERS is a Librarian for the Santa Clara County Library in California. She served four years on YALSA's Best DVDs and Videos for Young Adults Committee. She currently writes the "Teen Screen" video review column for *Voice of Youth Advocates* (*VOYA*).

FRANCISCA GOLDSMITH has been the Coordinator of Teen Services at Berkeley (California) Public Library since 1992. She is a past chair of YALSA's Audio Book and Media Exploration (formerly Media Selection and Usage) Committee. She has lots of ideas, and is lucky to work in a place that lets her try them out, even though she is sometimes cranky.

VALERIE A. OTT is the Teen Services Librarian at Wadsworth Public Library in Wadsworth, Ohio. She earned a bachelor's degree in English from Xavier University in 1998 and a master's degree in library and information science from Kent State University in 2001. Valerie is a member of the Ohio Library Council, ALA, and YALSA. As the Teen Services Librarian, she is the administrator of a grant aimed at promoting financial literacy to teens, funded by the Drew Carey Grant for Young Adult Services in Ohio.

MELANIE RAPP-WEISS is a Regional Teen Services Manager for Cuyahoga County (Ohio) Public Library. She was the 2002–2003 Chair of YALSA's Quick Picks for Reluctant Young Adult Readers Committee. Her ultimate goal in life is to be a backup singer for the Rolling Stones.

DAVID S. SERCHAY is a Youth Services Librarian for the Broward County (Florida) Library System. He has written on comics and graphic novels for a number of publications including *Library Journal, Comics*

Source, Animato, and *Serials Review.* On-line, he is a "founding member" of GN-LIB (a list for those interested in graphic novels and libraries) and a longtime participant in the Grand Comic Database Project (http://www.comics.org), an international on-line group dedicated to cataloging every comic book ever made. He has been reading comic books for most of his life, and has a personal collection of over 18,000 comics, dating back over 40 years.